REGIONAL ARCHAEOLOGIES **YORKSHIRE**

Frontispiece *Yorkshire with some of the major sites mentioned in the text*

REGIONAL ARCHAEOLOGIES

Yorkshire

BY I. H. LONGWORTH

CORY, ADAMS & MACKAY

Regional Archaeologies

GENERAL EDITOR: D. M. WILSON, M.A., F.S.A.
*Reader in Archaeology of the Anglo-Saxon Period at the University of London ;
President of the British Archaeological Association*

CONSULTANT EDITOR: A. D. ATIENZA, B.A. (Hons)
Deputy Head Teacher, Whitley Abbey Comprehensive School, Coventry

YORKSHIRE

© I. H. Longworth, 1965

The text is set in 'Monotype' Ehrhardt

First published 1965 by Cory, Adams & Mackay Ltd, 39 Sloane Street, London, SW1

Printed and bound in England by W. & J. Mackay & Co Ltd, Chatham, Kent

Contents

List of Illustrations

ACKNOWLEDGEMENTS

The author wishes to acknowledge his thanks to the following organizations and photographers for readily granting permission to reproduce the figures listed below: Mr S. W. Feather, F.S.A. SCOT., Keighley, Yorkshire, for fig. 21; F. Frith & Co. Ltd, Reigate, Surrey, for fig. 17; David S. Neal (1962 Crown Copyright Reserved) for fig. 43; The Royal Commission on Historical Monuments for fig. 41 (reproduced by permission of the Controller of Her Majesty's Stationery Office, Crown Copyright); Society of Antiquaries of London for fig. 37; The Trustees of the British Museum for figs. 20, 32, 33, 34, 38, and 45.

The author also wishes to record his warmest thanks to Mrs Eva Wilson, who has redrawn all the line illustrations; Mr I. M. Stead for reading through the text; and to acknowledge his very real debt to the many scholars and institutions whose original work has been adapted to the purposes of this book.

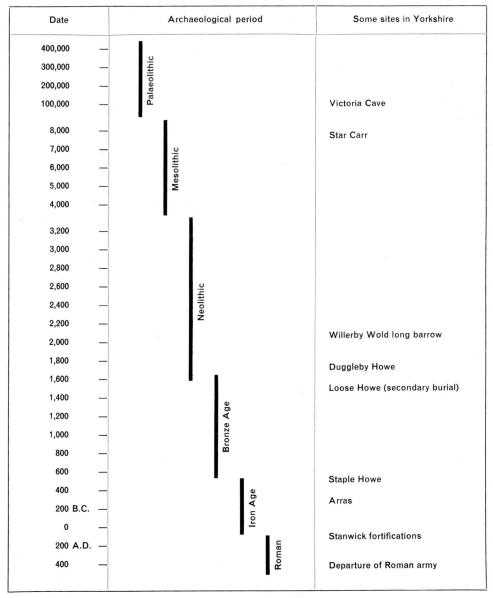

Date	Archaeological period	Some sites in Yorkshire
400,000 —	Palaeolithic	
300,000 —		
200,000 —		
100,000 —		Victoria Cave
8,000 —	Mesolithic	Star Carr
7,000 —		
6,000 —		
5,000 —		
4,000 —		
3,200 —	Neolithic	
3,000 —		
2,800 —		
2,600 —		
2,400 —		
2,200 —		
2,000 —		Willerby Wold long barrow
1,800 —		Duggleby Howe
1,600 —	Bronze Age	Loose Howe (secondary burial)
1,400 —		
1,200 —		
1,000 —		
800 —		
600 —		Staple Howe
400 —	Iron Age	Arras
200 B.C. —		
0 —		Stanwick fortifications
200 A.D. —	Roman	
400 —		Departure of Roman army

Fig. 1 *Dates, periods and sites*

The time scale in the left-hand column has been adjusted so that the divisions change from 100,000-year intervals during the long palaeolithic period to 1,000 years during the mesolithic and finally to 200 years from the neolithic onwards. This helps to show how swiftly the rate of change accelerates in Britain, once a basic knowledge of farming has been introduced.

1 Yorkshire and the First Hunters

Yorkshire, the largest county in the British Isles, is rich alike in natural beauty and in history. Within its boundaries lie high hills and low river valleys, barren moors and rich pasturage. In the west the county is dominated by the Pennines, rising in places to a height of 2,000 feet. These hills form a natural barrier. Only a few river valleys like Wensleydale and Airedale offer an easy route into Westmorland, Lancashire, and the west.

Between the Pennines and the north Yorkshire moors, running down the centre of the county, lies the broad valley of the Vale of York. To the north-east the peat-clad moors rise again to over 1,000 feet, broken here and there by steep-sided fertile valleys running north and south deep into the heart of the moors.

South of the moors and separating them from the chalk downs of the 'wolds' lies the Vale of Pickering. In the east this valley opens out on the coast at Filey Bay. Thirty miles away at its western end it joins the Vale of York through the narrow Coxwold-Gilling gap. Farther south lie the chalk lands of the wolds split into two arms; one stretching south to the River Humber; the other stretching eastwards towards the coast and ending in Flamborough Head. Between the two arms lies the low but undulating plain of Holderness bounded by the sea in the east and the River Humber in the south.

With its long coastline, Yorkshire received many settlers from across the North Sea. Other settlers followed the natural high road of the Jurassic ridge from the south. Few came from the west, where the Pennines barred the way, but through the Pennine passes flowed a steady stream of trade linking Yorkshire with the west and Ireland beyond. This book briefly sketches the history of the settlers and traders who came to make their home in Yorkshire. It tells of changing habits and new skills, moving from the simple but desperate life of the first hunters of the palaeolithic to the end of the Roman military occupation. Here one can offer no more than a quick guide to some of the more interesting discoveries which have been made. To fill out the picture one must visit the museums where much of the evidence—the tools and weapons, ornaments and cooking-pots—is now preserved. The country-side, too, preserves the past and many of the sites to be described well repay a visit. It is to the history of this country-side that we must now first turn.

ICE AND ITS EFFECTS

The hills and valleys which we see today began to take their final shape during the *Glacial Period*. The huge sheets of ice which formed during the intensely cold spells of this phase cut and reshaped the whole country-side with their weight and pressure. Though often termed the *Great Ice Age*, this was not a single period of extreme cold. At least four major cold spells have been recognized, but the intervals between them were warm. In fact, in these inter-glacial periods the climate was at times warmer than it is today. Hippopotamus and straight-tusked elephant are known to have roamed the Yorkshire country-side, for their bones have been found in Kirkdale Cave near Kirby Moorside.

In the cold spells much of Yorkshire was covered with ice. Ice from the north-east spread over the Yorkshire coast and the low-lying plain of Holderness, bringing with it rocks of Scandinavian origin. Another sheet of ice, stemming from the Pennines and the North of England, came down the Vale as far as the modern city of York. This brought with it boulders of Shap granite and Permian Brockram from the Vale of Eden. The material torn up in this way was dragged many miles before being redeposited when the ice began to melt. New surface deposits were built up with the broken rocks and finer clays which the glaciers left behind. By the action of winter frost and summer heat these were slowly turned into various types of soil. These in turn were to suit different kinds of trees and plants and often helped, as we shall see, to govern the areas where early man could make his home.

THE FIRST HUNTERS
OF THE PALAEOLITHIC

Man was at first a hunter, surviving by his skill in tracking down and killing the animals on which he fed. During the warmer spells of the glacial period he could no doubt have gathered a few fruits and nuts, but his staple diet was meat. His tools and weapons were simple, made from natural materials readily adapted to do basic jobs. His three main raw materials were stone, bone, and wood, and of these stone was the most important. It is for this reason that the earliest period of man's existence has been termed 'the palaeolithic' from two Greek words *palaios* and *lithos* meaning old stone—the Old Stone Age (fig. 1).

Flint was the most favoured stone, as it could readily be split. A lump of flint can be shaped by striking off a number of thin flat pieces or 'flakes'. The most widespread early form of tool in western Europe, a simple pointed implement called a *hand-axe*, was

made in this way. One of these was found many years ago at Huntow, near Bridlington, and is illustrated in figure 2 (no. 6). The hand-axe must have been to palaeolithic man hammer, scraper, and knife all rolled into one. But though it could be put to many simple uses it was still a clumsy tool. Not surprisingly, from an early date man also made use of the flakes which were detached from the larger lumps of flint. These could be worked into more delicate tools. By the late, or upper, palaeolithic man had acquired great skill in flint working and now concentrated on producing a long thin flake known as a blade. These blades could in turn be worked to make a range of specialized tools. The ends of some were trimmed to an even semicircle to form *scrapers* (fig. 2, no. 2) for cleaning the insides of animal hides. Some were worked into *awls* (fig. 2, no. 3)—pointed implements used for boring holes in skins so that they could be stitched together. Others were made into *burins* (fig. 2, no. 1), which were used for scratching deep grooves in bone and antler, from which splinters could be detached and made into pins and spearheads. Some of the narrow flint blades were also used as knives (fig. 2, no. 4).

The makers of these blade tools belong to the family of man called *Homo sapiens* and are the direct ancestors of modern man. They already show, though in a primitive form, the resourcefulness which allowed man to adapt himself to changing conditions of climate and landscape. His new tools allowed him to produce much finer implements in bone and antler than his predecessors, and besides being a tool-maker, he was also an impressive artist. To this upper palaeolithic period belongs the great cave art of France and Spain. Yet, despite these advances in skill and self-expression, upper palaeolithic man was still entirely dependent upon nature and upon the animals which he hunted. Most of his time

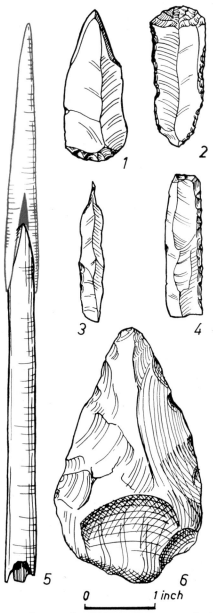

was spent in this search for food and much of the cave art was inspired by this ever-present need.

During the cold spells at least the North of England must have been an unattractive place in which to live. A few palaeolithic hunters are known to have sheltered for a time in the caves of Creswell Crags in Derbyshire, for they left behind their tools of stone and bone as well as the remains of the animals on which they fed. They must have been few in number and no comparable sites have yet been found in Yorkshire. A handful of stray flint implements, lost perhaps on hunting expeditions, do show, however, that man had already entered the region during the earlier part of the palaeolithic period. Three bone implements of the upper palaeolithic have also been found in a cave in the West Riding.

VICTORIA CAVE

Victoria Cave lies at a height of about 1,400 feet in a cliff of carboniferous limestone known as Kings Scar, not far from the town of Settle. The cave has three large irregular chambers with a single entrance facing south-west. In the earth at the mouth of the cave were found two pieces of reindeer antler. Both had been shaped into cylindrical rods, and one had been cut at one end from either side to form a double bevel. This probably formed the base of a spearhead, fitting into a forked joint (*see* fig. 2, no. 5), for it resembles a type of weapon made by upper palaeolithic man of the Magdalenian tradition, whose territory was centred on France and northern Spain. Another antler point, decorated with incised wavy lines, was found inside the cave. These three bone implements show that the direct ancestors of modern man had reached Yorkshire by about 10000 B.C.

Fig. 2 *Some palaeolithic implements: 1 burin, 2 scraper, 3 awl, 4 knife, 5 antler spearhead, restored point in red, 6 hand-axe*

THE POST-GLACIAL PERIOD

As the climate improved the ice-sheets slowly

began to retreat for the last time. The warmer conditions once more favoured the growth of vegetation, and along with new trees, shrubs and plants came new forms of animal life. This rebirth of vegetation can be traced in detail by means of *Pollen Analysis*.

Much of the pollen produced by plants and trees for the fertilization of their own species falls to the ground and becomes mixed with the soil around them. In favourable conditions, in the mud at the bottom of a lake, for instance, or in a peat bog, this pollen can survive for thousands of years. As the deposit at the bottom of the lake slowly builds up over the years, so each successive layer preserves pollen from the vegetation which surrounds the lake at the time when the layer was forming. Analysis of the pollen grains in samples of soil taken from each of these layers enables the botanist to construct a picture of the changes in vegetation in a particular area over a long period of time.

Analyses of samples taken from Star Carr, Flixton, and Killerby Carr in the Vale of Pickering trace the changing vegetation in east Yorkshire in the post-glacial period. With the final retreat of the ice-sheets the land became an open tundra covered with small patches of moss and lichen and an occasional dwarf shrub. This tundra slowly gave way to birch woods. Then pine trees joined the birch, and later still the country-side was covered with a mixed woodland of birch, pine, and hazel. At the height of the new warm spell a mixed oak forest, consisting of oak, elm, lime, and alder, replaced the pine and hazel. Only when the climate once again began to deteriorate, and inroads had been made on the forest with axe and fire, did the thick oak forest finally begin to disappear. These different phases can be seen in figure 3.

These changes in climate and vegetation also produced great changes in the animal population. The reindeer, who had thrived in the open late glacial tundra conditions, just as they do today in the Arctic, moved northwards as the ice receded. In their place came the *Aurochs*, an extinct form of wild ox, elk, red and roe deer, and wild pig, which were more suited to the new forest conditions.

MESOLITHIC MAN

These changes in climate and vegetation forced the hunters living near the edge of the receding ice-sheets to modify their way of life. Lacking domesticated animals and the skills needed to grow their own food, they were still compelled to feed themselves by hunting and fishing, though the opportunities for gathering nuts and fruits to supplement their diet were now greater. To meet the new conditions new tools and new forms of weapons were developed. Composite implements were made of flints set into wood and bone to form barbed spears and arrow-shafts. Hunters living near lakes and meres developed fish spears, or 'leisters', formed of two or more barbed points lashed together on the end of a long shaft. To combat the new growth of trees the axe and adze were devised; the axe to fell and trim the tree, the adze to hollow out and shape the timber. Of all man's tools the axe was to prove the most decisive in his struggle to overcome his natural surroundings.

This period of adaptation has been called the *Mesolithic*, or Middle Stone Age, for in many parts of Europe these new forms of stone and bone tools date to a phase which is later than the old hunters of the palaeolithic, but still earlier than the farmers of the succeeding neolithic or New Stone Age.

About 7500 B.C. a small band of these mesolithic hunters and fishers entered Yorkshire from the north-east over the marshy wastes of what is now the North Sea. This date was obtained by means of the *Carbon 14 dating method*. All living things absorb a radioactive substance known as Carbon 14. When

Pollen Zone	Main vegetation	
I	Grass and sedge	
II	Grass and sedge with some trees, especially birch	
III	Grass and sedge with some trees	
IV	Birch woods	
IV/V	Birch woods with some hazel and increasing number of pine trees	STAR CARR SETTLEMENT
V	Birch, pine and hazel woodland	
VI	Mixed oak forest, including oak, elm, lime, hazel and some alder	
VII	Rapid increase in alder	

Fig. 3 *Main changes in vegetation in East Yorkshire during early post-glacial times*

the organism dies no further Carbon 14 is absorbed and what remains in the body begins slowly to decay. By measuring the amount of radio-activity remaining in the specimen and comparing this with the radio-activity in modern carbon it is possible to estimate quite accurately the date when the organism died. This new band of hunters made their winter camp at Star Carr near Seamer and it was from birch wood found on this site that the date of 7538 ± 350 B.C. was obtained.

STAR CARR

It was the quick and experienced eye of a local man, Mr John Moore, which first spotted the decayed remains of bone and antler exposed in a field ditch at Star Carr—a vital clue to what lay beneath the peaty soil. The excavations, carried out by Professor Clark of Cambridge University, revealed a vivid picture of what a temporary camp of a group of mesolithic hunters was really like. When the ice-sheets covering northern Yorkshire began to melt a vast lake had formed in what is now the Vale of Pickering. This lake had gradually drained away, leaving behind a series of shallow meres and patches of marshland in its place. It was on the northern shore of one of these meres that the hunters had made their camp.

A rough platform of birch brushwood had been laid down and at one point two trees had been placed at right-angles to the platform out into the water to provide a rough landing-stage. Though it is likely that some sort of hut or shelter would have been erected on the platform, no trace remained. The camp covered an area of about 240 square yards and was probably occupied by a group of three or four families during the winter months and early spring for several years.

Fortunately for the archaeologist, prehistoric man was not a very tidy soul. Things which were broken or dropped usually remained where they had fallen, so that on a camping-site like Star Carr, where the bone and organic material is well preserved, a remarkably full picture of the life of the community could be obtained. The finds show quite clearly how much of mesolithic man's existence must have been taken up in the quest for food. Meat was still the main source of nourishment, and from the bones of the animals which the hunters had killed and brought back to their camp we know that red deer was the main object of their hunting expeditions. Bones of this animal were one and a half times as numerous as all the other animals put together. Then in order of importance came the wild ox (or *Bos primigenius* to give it its full Latin name), followed by elk, roe deer, and wild pig.

Despite the fact that the hunters were living beside a lake, bones of water-fowl and other birds are very few in number and there is no direct evidence of fishing. No fish bones were found but these are too small and soft to survive well under any conditions and there is plenty of evidence amongst the weapons found on the site that fishing must have played an important part in their life.

The people of Star Carr did not just eat the meat and throw away the bones and skins of the animals they had caught. These were far too valuable a source of raw materials for making other things. The antlers of red deer, and to some extent elk, were especially useful. Using a flint burin (fig. 4a, no. 2) to cut deep parallel grooves, long splinters were detached from the red-deer antler and made into barbed spearheads (fig. 4a, no. 1). A simple form of hoe or mattock (fig. 4a, no. 6) was made from elk antler and was used no doubt for grubbing up edible roots. Leg bones were also made into hollow tools which could be used along with the flint scrapers (fig. 4a, no. 4) for dressing skins. These tools and the flint awls (fig. 4a, no. 3) are clear evidence that the hunters and their wives wore skin clothing, though none of this survives.

Besides scrapers, burins and awls, flint was also used to make axes and adzes (fig. 4a, no. 5). The two trees which formed the primitive landing-stage showed clear signs that axes had been used to fell them. No boat was found, but a wooden paddle was discovered and no doubt the hunters had a canoe, made from a split tree trunk and hollowed out by means of fire and the flint adzes. Flake knives were also made and small flint points and blades known as *microliths*.

'Microlith' means literally a 'small stone' and is a name given to the small pieces of flaked and trimmed flint used in the composite weapons and tools of the period. Many of the flints must have been used as barbs and tips for arrows (*see* fig. 5a, right). Again, these small flints tell us that the hunters possessed the bow, though no example was found on the site.

Particularly interesting were the rolls of birch bark found on the site. Birch bark produces a sticky pitch-like substance and the birch-bark rolls represent the raw material from which this pitch was made. This primitive glue was used, among other things, for attaching the small flints to their wooden arrow-shafts. Indeed, a fragment of flint was found with some birch pitch still attached to it.

Intriguing, too, are twenty stag *frontlets* (fig. 4b), preserving the stag's antlers still attached to part of the skull, but deliberately lightened and perforated so that the frontlet could be worn as a mask on the head. They were probably worn by the hunters as they stalked their quarry, and perhaps also in ritual dances before the hunters set off on their expeditions. Amongst modern primitive tribes belief in magic plays an important part in the hunter's life and controls many of his actions.

The evidence tells us very little of what the Star Carr campers looked like. Besides the skin clothing which would have been essential in the cold winters of this early post-glacial period, beads made of stone, perforated deer teeth and amber were worn. Their life, at least in winter, seems to have left little leisure time for devising other forms of decoration. While man remained dependent upon the whims of nature for his food, leisure must have been hard to win.

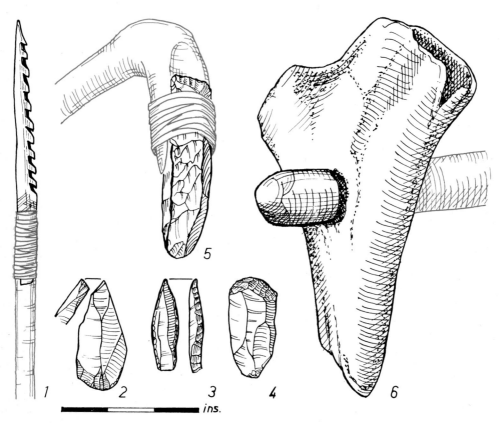

Fig. 4a *Mesolithic implements from Star Carr:* 1 *barbed antler spearhead,* 2 *burin,* 3 *awl,* 4 *scraper,* 5 *adze,* 6 *antler mattock (after Clark). Restored parts in red*

15

The hunters of Star Carr were proto-Maglemosians; that is to say they belong to a phase earlier than the Maglemosian hunters named after a site found in the Magle Mose ('Great Bog') near Mullerup in Zealand, Denmark. There are no settlements dating to this later phase in Yorkshire, although several typical spearheads have been found in the east of the county. Whereas the proto-Maglemosians of Star Carr used antler for their spearheads the Maglemosian harpoons are usually made of bone. They have been found at three sites all in the low-lying plain of Holderness, at Brandesburton, Hornsea, and Skipsea. Though most of the Maglemosian finds made so far in Yorkshire have been confined to the low-lying ground of east Yorkshire, these hunters certainly penetrated further inland. Two of their typical flint axes have been found in the West Riding: one at Rishworth in Calderdale and another on Blubberhouses Moor in mid-Wharfedale. Axes have also been found in the North Riding at Nova, near Pickering, and Cockheads in Glaisdale, as well as Skipsea in the south-east of the county.

THE HUNTERS OF THE MOORS

Some Maglemosian hunters are known to have lived on the high hills of the Pennines, and at Deepcar, the remains of flimsy shelter have been found. They made broad microlithic blades, often trimmed to form obliquely blunted points as well as burins and scrapers. To make points the micro-burin technique was often used. A pointed blade was selected and some way down a notch was chipped into the side (fig. 5a, left). This

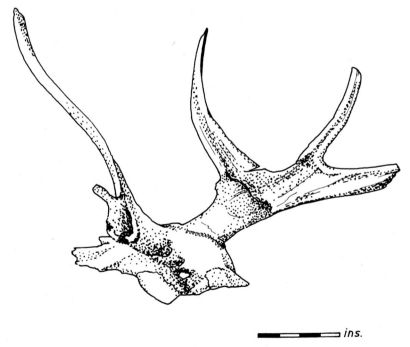

ins.

Fig. 4b *A Star Carr antler frontlet*

weakened the blade and with a quick twist the blade could be snapped in two. The point could then be used to tip or barb an arrow (fig. 5a, right) and the remaining portion thrown away. It is this second piece that has been called a 'micro-burin' because of its quite accidental likeness to the real graving tools known as burins.

Quite distinct from these Maglemosian hunters are a second group who lived both on the high hills of the Pennines and on the northern moors. They are related to the Sauveterrian hunters of France, named after

0   1 inch

Fig. 5b *Antler harpoon head from Victoria Cave*

the locality of Sauveterre-la-Lémance, Lot-et-Garonne. Their finds are especially common in the Marsden region, in the south-western corner of the county. The sites are usually found at a height of over 1,000 feet and comprise areas of worked flints often associated with hearths. These are the remains of temporary camps where the hunters sat round a fire to make a new set of microlithic-flint points and barbs for their arrows. They usually lie on a sandy layer overgrown by the more modern blanket peat bog and are particularly numerous along the narrow ridge from Stand Edge to Blackstone Edge.

These hunters made narrow-bladed microliths and these were worked into geometric shapes like triangles, crescents, and trapezes, which could then be used as points

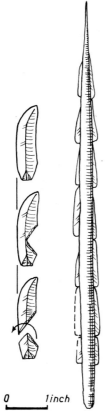

0   1 inch

Fig. 5a *The microburin technique (left) and composite arrow-shaft (right)*

and barbs inset into arrow-shafts. The micro-burin technique was again often used. Similar narrow-bladed microliths have been found on the Cleveland Hills, on the moors between Hawnby and Chopgate in Bilsdale, on Brown Hill, Commondale, between Glaisdale and Rosedale, and on Danby Low Moor.

One further find deserves mention, for it points to further discoveries which may be made in the future. In the same cave that yielded the Magdalenian bone implements of the upper palaeolithic phase, Victoria Cave near Settle, a stag-antler harpoon was found. This harpoon is of a distinctive shape (fig. 5b), broad with barbs on either side. In form it is very similar to the Azilian harpoons of northern Spain, named after the cave of Mas d'Azil in the Pyrenees, and to harpoons found in north-west Scotland. This find suggests that yet another distinct group of hunters had entered Yorkshire during this period. Perhaps some day a cave in the lime-stone areas of the West Riding will provide more information about their way of life.

2 *The First Farmers*

THE NEAR EAST

Already by 8000 B.C. man had built his first town. Recent excavations at the site of Jericho, which lies to the north of the Dead Sea, revealed a community living within stout defensive walls. Many layers of occupation debris had accumulated before the stage dated by Carbon 14 to 8200 B.C. A site like Jericho implies a settled community, and though gazelle were still being hunted in large numbers these early town dwellers had pro-bably acquired some of the basic skills of farming. By 6000 B.C. it is almost certain that over wide areas of the Near East man had learnt to sow cereal grains like barley and wheat and reap the crop later in the year when the grain was ripe. From an early stage, too, he had tamed both sheep and goat and probably cattle. These first farmers belong to the *neolithic* or New Stone Age, but though the farmers developed new forms of stone tools, as the name implies, it is not so much these as the basic knowledge of farming which forms the most important feature of this 'neolithic' period.

The change from hunting to farming was neither swift nor complete, but it was momen-tous. The rising temperatures of the early post-glacial period and the melting of the ice-sheets had had a profound effect upon the climate of the world. While the hunters of Star Carr were stalking red deer in the birch woods of east Yorkshire, the lands bordering the eastern Mediterranean had already begun to feel the effects of a greatly reduced rain-fall. As the countryside changed, men living in these regions were forced to rely less on hunting and find new ways to supplement their diet. The change from hunting to farm-ing was a tremendous step forward in man's struggle with nature, but it was a slow process. For many communities hunting was still a necessary part of life for centuries to come.

BRITAIN

Many miles lie between these earliest neolithic farming communities of the Near East and Britain, and it took over three thousand years for the new-found knowledge of farming to reach Yorkshire. Small groups of farmers began to reach the shores of Britain two or three centuries before 3000 B.C. They practised mixed farming, growing cereals and herding cattle. Sheep, goats, and pigs all had a place on these first British farms.

The new immigrants brought with them a knowledge of how to make pottery. Their pots are, by modern standards, crude and rather drab. The basic shape was a simple bowl, sometimes globular with a small mouth, sometimes shallow and open. A few have 'lugs'—pieces of clay attached to the surface and pierced so that a string could be passed through them. This allowed the pot to be carried more securely and hung up when not in use. The colour of the pots does not vary much and is nearly always muddy brown. Many were left completely plain, though the surface of some has been carefully smoothed. When decoration does occur the patterns are simple and usually made with a finger-nail or something that came readily to hand, like the end of a twig or a bird bone.

Pollen analysis shows that the farmers were moving into a land which was in parts thickly wooded. They avoided the valleys and the heavy clay lands which at this period carried a thick, damp, mixed oak forest. Instead they chose the chalk downs, gravels, and sandy heaths where the woodlands were much lighter and more open. When small groups moving northwards from southern England finally reached Yorkshire they naturally settled mainly on the wolds and limestone hills of eastern Yorkshire.

In southern England causewayed camps were built—like that on Windmill Hill, near Avebury in Wiltshire. These camps are circular and surrounded by ditches, which are broken up into short segments by unexcavated causeways. It is this distinctive feature which gives the monuments their name. The majority are not really farms but market places where groups of farmers met, brought their surplus cattle and exchanged their wares. The farmers lived elsewhere. At Haldon, in Devon, a large rectangular house 25 feet long and 16 feet wide was found. The walls were supported by stout timber posts and the house had a gabled roof. In one corner was a hearth and scattered over the floor in two distinct layers separated by wind-blown sand lay domestic refuse including pieces of the typical pottery of the early farmers. Here was an isolated farmhouse which had been occupied, left for a while, and then reoccupied probably by the same group of people.

The farmers did not always live in such isolation. At Hurst Fen near Mildenhall in Suffolk a number of families lived together on a piece of sandy heathland, but their huts or shelters must have been very flimsy affairs. All that remained for the archaeologist were clusters of pits, once used perhaps for storing grain and later filled up with household rubbish including broken pots, flint scrapers, discarded arrowheads and a great number of waste flakes.

These are the sort of huts and settlements which are likely to be found some day in Yorkshire. But at present we must be content with less satisfactory sites. On Beacon Hill, Flamborough Head, the farmers certainly stayed long enough to break a pot or two, but no trace of a hut was found. No doubt the Yorkshire farms remain undiscovered because they have left little indication of their presence on the surface of the ground. Their burial places, however, are more easily found, for the farmers considered it fitting to make the last resting-place of their dead conspicuous for all to see.

LONG BARROWS

Most of the domestic pottery known from Yorkshire in this period has been found not in settlements but with burials or beneath the great mounds which were built over them. The farmers took great care in burying their dead and, just as today, not all groups agreed on the way this should be done. Some thought the dead should be buried unburnt, others cremated their dead, but most seem to have agreed that a long mound was a fitting monument to erect over them. It is these long barrows which give us some indication of where the farmers were actually living in the county.

At least twenty-three long barrows have been found in eastern Yorkshire (fig. 6). They are scattered over the chalk wolds, from Market Weighton in the south to Folkton in the east, and others have been found along the limestone hills north of the Vale of Pickering, near Seamer, Ebberston, Cropton, and Kilburn. Three are also known in the north-east; Lingrow Howe, Birkdale, and on Sleights Moor in lower Eskdale. Only one long barrow has been found high up on the moors (on Kepwick Moor in the Hambleton Hills). These long barrows fall into two main groups; those which cover unburnt bodies (inhumations) and those which contain cremation deposits.

All the long barrows covering unburnt bodies so far examined were excavated in the nineteenth century. They were opened by local antiquaries like the Rev. William Greenwell, later Canon of Durham Cathedral, who gave his collections to the British Museum, and John Mortimer of Driffield, whose collection can now be seen in Hull. Though these early excavators recorded many of the things they found and saw, they took less trouble over their work than is required today, and our best picture of one of these mounds is provided by the Giants' Hills long barrow near Skendleby on the Lincolnshire wolds excavated by Mr C. W. Phillips during 1933 and 1934.

GIANTS' HILLS LONG BARROW

This mound (fig. 7, left) was 200 feet long, but ploughing had reduced its height down to only 5 feet. The soil and chalk for its construction were obtained from ditches dug around the sides. The burials lay at the eastern end of the barrow on a narrow pavement of chalk slabs set at right-angles to the main axis of the barrow. There were eight skeletons but only five still lay with their bones in the correct order (*articulated*). The bones of the other three were confused and, on closer examination, showed signs of

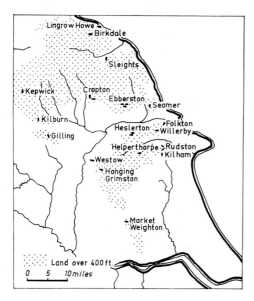

Fig. 6 *Distribution of long barrows in East Yorkshire (after Manby)*

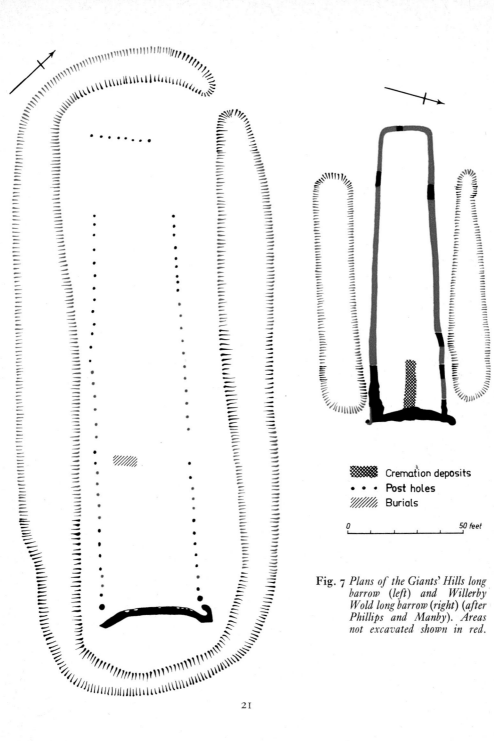

Cremation deposits

• • • Post holes

/////// Burials

0   50 feet

Fig. 7 *Plans of the Giants' Hills long barrow (left) and Willerby Wold long barrow (right) (after Phillips and Manby). Areas not excavated shown in red.*

weathering. More interesting still was the discovery inside one of the skulls of an egg-case belonging to a snail of a type which lays its eggs only in the open and never underground.

Three conclusions could immediately be drawn from this evidence. Firstly, the mound had only been built after eight people belonging probably to the same group had died. Secondly, three of the bodies had decayed so far that their bones were no longer held together by sinews. Thirdly, wherever the bodies had been stored they had not been buried in the ground, but had been open to the air and had suffered from the weather. The final piece of evidence came from the barrow itself. Within the mound traces of upright timbers were found forming a rough rectangle—189 feet by 37 feet. The uprights had been placed every 5 feet along the sides, but at the eastern end split logs had been set upright and close together in a narrow trench to form a rough crescent. At the western end eight upright posts had been set in the ground, symbolizing perhaps the eight burials. Traces were also noticed of turfs placed round the burials. Here, then, was a piece of ground marked off by upright timbers within which successive bodies had been placed until the time came for the mound to be built. The barrow had been built, in fact, over a mortuary enclosure.

The long mound at Hanging Grimston, examined by Mortimer, probably contained one of these enclosures, and another at Gilling certainly did. The long barrow at Kilham had at least nine articulated skeletons scattered along its length, lying on the old ground surface beneath the mound. But this habit of storing the dead in mortuary enclosures is not confined to the inhumation long barrows, for Mr Manby of the Tolson Memorial Museum, Huddersfield, has recently excavated one of the cremation long barrows on Willerby Wold and found much the same story there.

THE WILLERBY WOLD LONG BARROW

This barrow lies at the eastern end of Willerby Wold, above the hamlet of Fordon, about 7 miles south of Scarborough. Mr Manby found that this massive mound (fig. 7, right), 122 feet long and 35 feet broad, had been built over a trapezoidal-shaped mortuary enclosure. At the eastern end a concave row of upright posts had been set into a narrow trench similar to the one in the Giants' Hills long barrow. Unlike that barrow, the Willerby posts had been deliberately burnt down before the mound had been erected. But the main interest of the Willerby barrow is that it has been built like a lime kiln.

At the eastern end of the mound the remains of a number of disarticulated skeletons had been placed on the old ground surface. Then blocks of chalk and flint had been stacked over them mixed with lengths of timber in such a way that air could get through to the wood. The mound had then been erected and this *crematorium* deposit fired. The heat of the fire turned the chalk blocks into lime and the human bones were cremated.

At least eight long barrows of this *Crematorium* type are known in Yorkshire and they are confined to the county with the single exception of one at Crosby Garrett in Westmorland. This was an important discovery, for it shows that not all the farmers who reached Yorkshire were content to remain in the county. Some clearly felt the need to find new ground and set off to cross the Pennines probably by way of Swaledale and so reach the Eden Valley, and eventually, the Irish Sea.

MEGALITHIC TOMBS

In northern and western Britain long mounds were often built over burial chambers made out of large stone slabs, or *megaliths*. Unlike the earth mounds just described, these were collective tombs and could be reopened each time a body was to be placed in one of the burial chambers. The builders of these great megalithic chambered tombs do not seem to have entered Yorkshire, unless the long barrow on Bradley Moor, north-west of Keighley, is a late example of their work. The mound is about 230 feet long and excavations revealed a stone cist, 6½ feet long and 3 feet wide, some 60 feet from the eastern end of the barrow. The cist, a sort of stone box, was formed by four slabs of stone set on end with a fifth forming a 'capstone' or lid. A sixth slab lay on the floor and this covered a deposit of unburnt but smashed human bones. Cremated bones were also found in the cist. Besides this grave other upright stones were covered by the mound, but these served no particular function.

POTTERY

The type of domestic pottery found in and beneath the long barrows has a distinctive 'Yorkshire' appearance. There are two main styles and both have been named after barrows in which they were well represented. Bowls of *Grimston Ware* (fig. 8, no. 1) are well made and of fine texture, usually with an out-turned rim and a 'carination' or shoulder. In contrast, bowls of *Heslerton Ware* (fig. 8, no. 2) are coarser with a rolled-over rim and S-profile. Simple round-based open bowls are also found.

FARMING TOOLS AND WEAPONS

The hewn timbers found in the long barrows show that the farmers were already accomplished lumbermen and the axe must have been an indispensable tool at this stage for making clearings in the woodland. The earliest farmers in Britain used both flint and stone axes and these were soon to be traded over

long distances. Large flint-mines were dug in the chalk lands of southern England at sites like Grimes Graves, near Weeting in Norfolk, and Cissbury in Sussex to obtain the raw material. In the north and west of Britain stone-axe *'factories'* were set up in Great Langdale in Westmorland and at Graig Lwyd in North Wales. At these sites, usually found on the slopes of the hills where suitable stone

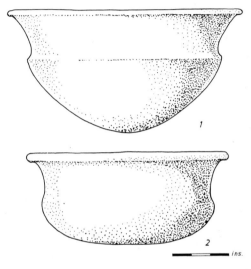

Fig. 8 *Neolithic bowls from:* 1 *Hanging Grimston*, 2 *Heslerton*

outcropped and could readily be quarried, large numbers of stone axes were roughed out, and then taken away to be finished off elsewhere.

Clearings were made in the woods by burning and cutting down the trees, but the roots were probably left in the ground. Having no plough, which would in any case have been quickly broken in the uncleared ground, the farmers raked their seeds into the top soil with a simple hoe. From finds of accidentally burnt grain and impressions

23

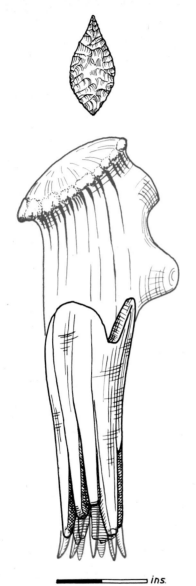

Fig. 9 *Leaf shaped arrowhead (above) from Tow-*
thorpe, and antler comb (below) from Garton
Slack, restored parts in red

of grains incorporated into the pottery, we know that the chief crops were wheat and barley. Herds of cattle would have provided skins for clothing as well as food, and flint scrapers for cleaning the hides are common. But hunting still played a useful part in providing food for the home.

One of the most characteristic flint implements made by the farmers throughout southern and eastern England was the leaf-shaped arrowhead (fig. 9, above). The woodlands provided a fair range of game from the mighty *Bos primigenius*, red and roe deer, wild horse to wild pig. Like the mesolithic hunters described in the last chapter, the farmers of the neolithic made use of the skins and bones of these animals as well as eating their flesh. The antlers of the red deer were now used for making antler hoes and 'picks', which might be more correctly described as levers. The great long mounds of chalk could not have been built without these 'picks', which were hammered into cracks in the chalk and then used to lever out the blocks. Antler was also used for making rough combs, not for human hair but to strip the outer hair from hides. One of these antler combs (fig. 9, below) was found with a bowl of *Grimston Ware* in a hole beneath a round barrow in Garton Slack.

Wood does not preserve well on the chalk and limestone unless it has been burnt, but the flint arrowheads must have had shafts and there must have been bows to fire them. The axes, too, would have required hafts. Two neolithic bows recently discovered during peat cutting at Ashcott and Meare in Somerset can be dated by Carbon 14 to 2665 and 2690 $\pm$ 120 B.C. respectively. As for axe hafts, a lakeside camp at Ehenside Tarn in Cumberland produced an axe still in its beech-wood haft.

3 Native and New-comer

A TIME OF CHANGE—THE LATE NEOLITHIC

Many centuries after the arrival of the first farmers in Britain new types of pottery and new forms of stone and bone implement gradually came into use. In southern England the causewayed camps and the long barrows cease to be built and a variety of new forms of burial rite appear. By 2000 B.C. more immigrants had begun to arrive on our southern and eastern shores. In Yorkshire the early farmers seem to have retained their traditions and customs much longer than in southern England, for many of the new types of pottery, implements, and burial customs appear alongside their simple bowls and beneath their long barrows. The late neolithic is a period of variety in which old and new become intermingled. The burial mound at Duggleby Howe belongs to this phase.

DUGGLEBY HOWE

Duggleby Howe is a round barrow, southeast of the modern village of Duggleby. The mound is a massive 120 feet in diameter and still stands today 20 feet high, though originally it must have been at least 10 feet higher. At the centre a pit had been dug 9 feet into the chalk and at the bottom of this an adult male had been buried with a pottery bowl of the sort found in the long barrows. The pit had then been filled with chalk rubble and further bodies of adults and children. Next to this pit a shallow grave had then been dug for two skeletons. With one had been placed a bone skewer pin, five chisel-ended arrowheads, boars' tusk blades, beavers' teeth and flint flakes. With the other was a fine polished flint knife.

Above the filled-in central pit another male body had been buried with an antler 'macehead', a chipped and polished flint axe and lozenge-shaped arrowhead. All these burials lay beneath a mound of rubble 50 feet in diameter, containing another five inhumations. But amongst this rubble, and in a chalky rubble layer above, had been inserted at least fifty cremations, four accompanied by bone pins. These bone skewer pins (fig. 10, no. 3) were probably used to secure the bag in which the ashes had been collected, though all trace of the bag itself had rotted away. The whole of this mound was later given a further capping of chalk rubble and would then no doubt have gleamed white in the sun—an impressive monument by any standards.

The Duggleby mound is curious. It is round, not long, and the burials placed beneath it are a mixture of inhumations and cremations. Some of the inhumations have been given individual burial, but others have been buried in groups, showing that the storage of dead bodies was still being practised. The cremation burials are quite different affairs from the 'lime-kiln' burials beneath the long barrows. The Duggleby Howe cremations consist of heaps of bones collected from funeral pyres which were built elsewhere.

The objects with these burials give a fair idea of the range of new tools and weapons now being made. The flint axes (fig. 10, no. 5) are now often long and thin and sometimes 'waisted'. Their cutting edges have been sharpened not by chipping but by grinding —a technique really developed for sharpen-

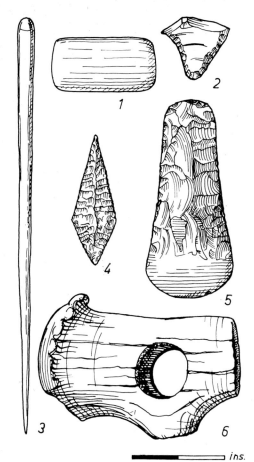

heads, to give them their technical name) were made from a segment of a blade, the sides and butt being trimmed for hafting, but one long edge left sharp to form the cutting edge. The 'maceheads' (fig. 10, no. 6) show that antler was still being used, though the maces themselves are more likely to be symbols of authority than offensive weapons.

A similar set of objects was placed with a deposit of human bones beneath a flat stone in the long barrow at East Ayton near Scarborough. Here four polished flint axes, five lozenge-shaped arrowheads, two flint knives, one with a polished cutting edge, two boars' tusk blades and another antler macehead had been placed with the bones.

PETERBOROUGH WARE

Flint knives with polished edges have also been found elsewhere with a highly decorated type of pottery known as Peterborough Ware, named after a site at Peterborough in Northamptonshire. The earliest Peterborough bowls, though often decorated, are not unlike the round-based pots made by the first farmers, but gradually more specialized forms were developed. These later bowls (fig. 11) are usually decorated with simple repetitive patterns impressed with a whipped or twisted

Fig. 10 *Late Neolithic implements: 1 polished flint knife, 2 chisel-ended arrowhead and 3 bone skewer pin, from Duggleby Howe, 4 lozenge shaped arrowhead, 5 waisted axe and 6 antler 'macehead', from East Ayton*

ing stone axes. Some of the flint knives have their edges ground in the same way (fig. 10, no. 1). Flint arrowheads are often either chisel-ended (fig. 10, no. 2) or of lozenge shape (fig. 10, no. 4) with very fine flaking to reduce their thickness. These chisel-ended arrowheads (or *petit-tranchet derivative arrow-*

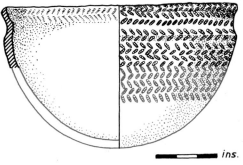

Fig. 11 *Bowl of Peterborough Ware from Thornton-le-dale (after Manby), restored base in red*

cord, or sometimes with the end of a small bird bone or twig or the end of a flint flake. The hollow neck often carries a row of finger-tip impressions and the rim is usually turned over into a protruding lip.

Peterborough Ware has been found on many sites in southern and eastern England. Many of the finds have come from rivers, like the complete bowl from the Thames at Mortlake, or from river valleys, suggesting that the Peterborough people often travelled by river. Peterborough Ware has also been found in several of the Pennine caves like Elbolton Cave near Thorpe in Wharfedale and Sewell's cave near Settle. The Peter-borough people seem to have taken part in the distribution of stone axes from both the Langdale and the Graig Lwyd axe factories and of flint axes from the Grimes Graves flint-mines in East Anglia. Their characteristic pottery was found together with a Langdale axe in the remains of a camp covered by a round barrow at North Deighton, north of Wetherby in the West Riding. Elsewhere in Yorkshire, Peterborough Ware has been found with simpler pottery, typical of the early farmers. One such site came to light through quarrying on the southern slope of the wide dry valley called Garton Slack, three miles west of Driffield. Here in a hollow between Craike Hill and a low hill to the south-west were found the remains of a camp fire sur-rounded by broken pots, including bowls of Grimston, Heslerton, and Peterborough Ware, together with fragments of a 'beaker'.

THE BEAKER PEOPLE

The *Beaker* found amongst the pottery at Craike Hill shows that a new set of immigrants had already arrived in Yorkshire. The new arrivals are known collectively as the Beaker people, but they came in small bands to many points along the coasts of southern and eastern Britain over a period of years from about 2000 to 1700 B.C. They came from different parts of the Rhineland and the Low Countries, but all possessed one thing in common; they all made, in one form or another, a beaker-shaped pot.

Many of these beakers show great skill in their manufacture and have been decorated with great care. The earliest arrivals from the Rhineland brought beakers with a flowing-S profile—looking like an upturned bell. Hence they have been given the name *Bell Beakers* (fig. 12, no. 1). They are decorated in hori-zontal zones, a decorated zone often alternat-ing with a plain zone. The patterns were usually produced by impressing a comb with rectangular teeth into the clay. Of similar shape, but decorated with horizontal lines made with a twisted cord, are the *Corded Beakers* (fig. 12, no. 4) brought by another group of immigrants who arrived about the same time. A later movement about 1700 B.C. brought people making pots with more angular profiles called *Short-necked Beakers* (fig. 12, no. 2), a form which developed in Holland from the earlier bell beakers. This last wave of Beaker settlers landed mainly in north-east Scotland, but a few came farther south. As well as introducing new tastes in pottery, these immigrants brought the custom of single burial to Britain.

SINGLE GRAVES AND ROUND BARROWS

The new immigrants usually buried their dead in a crouched position with their knees drawn up towards their chest and their hands before their face. Very often a round mound of earth was then heaped over the grave and, although these round barrows are by no means as large as the long mounds they are still im-pressive monuments. Beaker barrows occur frequently on the chalk wolds and limestone hills, but are rare on the northern moors and the Pennines. Clearly the new immigrants favoured the lighter soils and shunned the

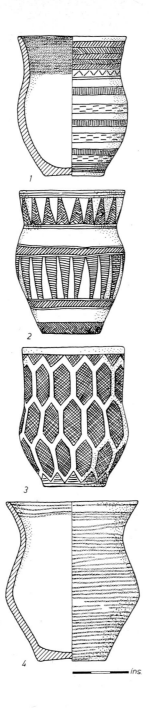

higher hills and river valleys which would still have carried a heavy forest cover. Some hardy travellers, however, used the Pennine passes and are buried with their pots, for example, on Baildon Moor, at Lea Green near Grassington in Wharfedale, and at Ferry Fryston.

Once in Britain the new immigrants developed a new type of pot, a *Long-necked Beaker* (fig. 12, no. 3). These are often decorated in panels, rather than zones, and comb impressions were now used to form quite complicated designs. These include lozenges, triangles, and lattice patterns, and 'reserved' patterns were often created by leaving parts of the surface undecorated to form a second pattern. Handled beakers were also occasionally made. A burial found beneath a round barrow on the farm of Kelleythorpe, near Driffield, excavated by Lord Londesborough in 1851, belongs to an early stage in this development.

At the centre of the barrow lay a stone cist composed of four upright slabs of stone with a cover stone lying at the level of the old ground surface. The cist had been paved with small irregular slabs. On this paving lay the skeleton of a man in a crouched position lying on his left side, his hands before his face. On his right forearm lay a curved stone wrist guard (fig. 13, no. 2), perforated at each corner for rivets which still retained their golden heads. A guard is used by archers to protect their wrists against the return of the bow string after the arrow has been released. Behind the spine lay a wooden-handled copper knife (fig. 13, no. 3) in a wooden sheath. Near his neck were three amber buttons, perforated for attachment by boring from two points to meet in a V (fig. 13, no. 1). These probably once fastened his linen tunic, though only a

Fig. 12 *Beakers: 1 Bell and 2 Short-necked, from Goodmanham, 3 Long-necked from Sharpe Howe, 4 Corded from Ashberry (after Hayes)*

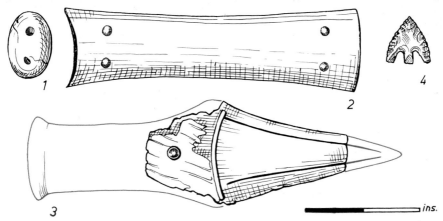

Fig. 13 1 *V-perforated amber button,* 2 *stone wrist guard and* 3 *copper knife (handle and tip restored in red),
from Kelleythorpe,* 4 *barbed and tanged flint arrowhead from Thwing*

trace of this survived. Behind the legs lay a
fine long-necked beaker, perhaps once containing a drink to sustain the dead man on
whatever journey he had now begun.

The man buried at Kelleythorpe may well
have been a renowned bowman in his day,
and it is significant that one of the commonest
flint implements associated with the Beaker
people was the *barbed and tanged flint arrowhead* (fig. 13, no. 4). Three of these were
found together in a grave beneath a round
barrow in the parish of Thwing. Hunting
must still have played an important part in
providing food for the home. But to judge
from impressions of grain accidentally pressed
into the surface of the pottery beakers while
they were being made, barley was now the
main cereal crop.

TRADE AND THE INTRODUCTION
OF COPPER AND BRONZE

The Kelleythorpe burial also illustrates two
important innovations. With the arrival of the
Beaker immigrants copper knives and awls
appear for the first time with the dead.
Secondly, the gold rivet heads on the stone

wrist guard and the amber buttons show that
our Beaker archer had a taste for fine things—
some of which were not readily to hand in
Yorkshire. In fact, both gold and amber were
probably brought to Yorkshire by trade: gold
from the Wicklow Mountains in Ireland, and
amber from the shores of the Baltic. The introduction of metal for tools and long-distance
trade were to form the essential basis of the
flourishing bronze-using culture of the succeeding period.

The first metal tools were, in fact, made of
copper not bronze, and the forms are very
simple. The axe, still the basic tool of a farming people, was flat—made by pouring molten
copper into an open stone mould. Copper
knives were made, some with an elongated
tang to help in attaching the handle of bone,
wood or horn. Others had the handle riveted
on, and some used both tang and rivet. The
small copper awls were set into wooden
handles as borers.

It was not long before true bronze was
being used for implements. Bronze is a mixture of copper and tin. By adding a small quantity of tin to the copper a tougher implement

29

can be produced, although if too much tin is added the metal becomes brittle: 10 per cent tin and 90 per cent copper are about the best proportions. The addition of tin also makes the pouring of molten metal into the mould much easier and this paved the way, as we shall see, for great advances in casting methods with more complex moulds. The first bronze implements, however, like the four flat axes (fig. 14, no. 4) from a barrow on Wold Farm, Willerby, are little different in form from the earlier copper tools.

The Beaker people's taste for fine objects is well illustrated by the magnificent knife and armlet found with a crouched burial in one of the round barrows of the Garton Slack group. The knife (fig. 14, no. 1) was 8 inches long. Its hilt was made of two plates of horn held together by forty-two rivets set in four rows, and was capped by a bone pommel. The hilt itself was riveted on to the metal blade. With the knife lay a metal armlet (fig. 14, no. 2) decorated with an incised lozenge design, and two thin rods bent at each end to form a hook. Nor is fine workmanship in the period confined to copper and bronze work. Gold is rare, but a pair of basket-shaped gold ear-rings (fig. 14, no. 3) were found by Mr Willmot of the Yorkshire Museum on the old ground surface sealed beneath the rampart of an Iron Age hill-fort at Boltby Scar. A similar pair have been found

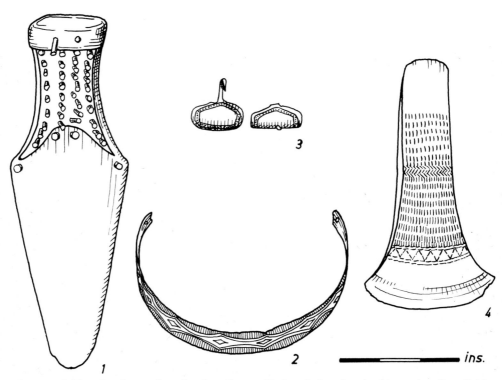

Fig. 14 1 *knife and* 2 *decorated armlet, from Garton Slack,* 3 *basket-shaped gold ear-rings from Boltby Scar,* 4 *decorated flat axe from Willerby Wold*

with a collared bell beaker at Radley in Berkshire. It was this Beaker taste for display which led to the first major working of jet in Yorkshire.

JET

Jet is a type of fossilized wood, black in colour, which occurs mainly in the Upper Lias Shales. It is found not in seams like coal but in individual lumps. These jet-bearing shales outcrop at a number of points along the north-east Yorkshire coast, at Peak, for example, and Saltwick Nab, Sandsend, and Runswick Bay. It was probably lumps washed out from these outcrops which first attracted prehistoric man to jet. Conical buttons, necklaces of beads and belt fasteners were all made in jet, and though many now on display in the museums have cracked with time and are very fragile, some still retain the qualities which made jet so attractive to the Beaker people and those who came after them.

Two conical buttons made of jet were found with a Beaker burial in a sandpit at Middleton-on-the-Wolds. The Beaker is a very fine one with comb-impressed decoration, and with it were three flints. One is a knife, $6\frac{1}{2}$ inches long, of black flint finely flaked on both sides. This clearly copies in flint one of the new flat metal knives, for metal tools were extremely rare and it was only natural that they should be copied in the more traditional flint. The second flint is a simple blade knife. The third, adhering to a piece of decomposed iron pyrites, was a bar of flint 3 inches long, which formed a simple strike-a-light. By striking the flint against the iron pyrites a spark could be readily produced.

A similar burial was found beneath one of the round barrows in the Garton Slack group. The skeleton lay with a long-necked beaker, a jet button, a flint and lump of iron pyrites and another fine flint copy of a metal knife.

With these was a stone battle-axe, pointed at one end, rounded at the other and perforated for hafting. The battle-axe is relatively rare in Britain, but was a favourite weapon amongst the late neolithic population of northern Europe.

THE WINDYPIT BURIALS

The most curious burials of the period were those found recently in the 'windypits', which lie in or near the valley of the River Rye between Duncombe Park and Arden, north-west of Hawnby. The Windypits are natural fissures probably made by the limestone and grit slipping on a band of clay. There are eight main fissures and Beakers have been found in four, Slip Gill, Antofts, Ashberry, and Buckland's. All are difficult to enter and require great skill to examine.

In the Antofts windypit (fig. 15), about 80 feet below the surface, was found a skull

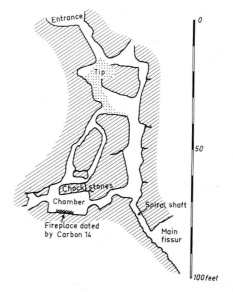

Fig. 15 *Section through the Antofts Windypit (after Hayes and Pacitto)*

31

and part of the skeleton of a middle-aged woman. They lay with other human and animal bones in a mass of stones at the top of a vertical shaft which from that point spirals downwards. Farther down the fissure a natural chamber was discovered floored by jammed boulders and roofed by a large slab, which had helped to keep the chamber dry. In the chamber a fire had been lit on a fallen block of limestone and around it lay the bones of an ox, which had been broken open to extract the marrow. Farther away were bones of pig and sheep and the jaw and skull of a badger. On the floor lay a flint knife and scraper and on the opposite side of the fissure, about 6 or 7 feet from the fire, lay a corded beaker. A sample taken from the fire gave a Carbon 14 date of 1790 ± 150 B.C. In all, the remains of eight persons were found in the fissure and fragments of four or five different beakers. There seems no doubt that this natural fissure had been used as a communal burial vault.

WHAT THE BURIALS SHOW

The burials just described give some idea of what the Beaker people wore and what they used. Temporary camps are known in Yorkshire, but sherds of broken pots and a few flint implements round the remains of an open fire tell us little of the people themselves. The skeletons show that some Beaker people had round heads, while others had longer skulls. Compared to the native population, they were probably bigger and stronger in physique. Their principal weapon was the bow, but some possessed the battle-axe. They were fine potters with an eye for symmetry and decoration and liked personal ornaments of exotic materials. They wove cloth and knew the value of the new metal tools. Yet basically they were farmers and shepherds and their bows were probably used as much in defence of their flocks as in seizing new land. As pioneers, traders, and farmers their influence quickly spread.

Such forceful new-comers naturally had great influence upon the native farming population. Old ideas were exchanged for new beliefs. The great mound at Duggleby may be a compromise between the old long barrow and the new, but usually much smaller, round barrow. A more obvious mixture of beliefs can be seen in round barrows raised above crematorium deposits similar to the one found beneath the Willerby Wold long barrow. Here the old burial beliefs persist, but the type of mound raised over the dead conforms with the new ideas brought in by the Beaker people.

HENGE MONUMENTS
AND STANDING STONES

To this period of changing beliefs belong some of the most puzzling monuments to be found in Britain. These are the *henge monuments*—circular ceremonial sites which take their name from Stonehenge. Round Ripon, between the Ure and the Swale, no less than six were built in an area only 7 miles long (fig. 16). Round the henges cluster twenty-eight round barrows and one can only assume that here was an important religious centre. As to what form the religion took there can be no definite answer, for the henge monuments yield little evidence. At Thornborough three huge henge monuments stand in line, half a mile apart, running roughly north-west and south-east. They are about 800 feet across, almost circular, and have two entrances, one leading into the circle on the north-west side, the other on the south-east. The circular area is enclosed by a bank which must have stood at least 10 feet high when first built. Ditches were dug both inside and outside the bank, over 60 feet wide and 8 to 10 feet deep. As the monument stands today the outer of the two ditches has been filled up with plough soil and is no longer

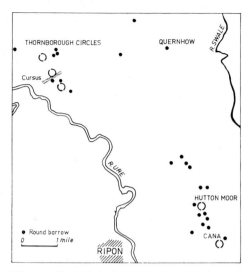

Fig. 16 *Map of the henge monuments and round barrows near Ripon (after Thomas)*

and, as in other cursus monuments in the county, were discovered from the air as two dark lines in the cereal crops. Where the crops lie over the ditch the greater moisture has caused them to grow taller. In this way the lines of the ditches stand out in the crops, though it is usually difficult to pick them out from the ground. The cursus, like the henge monument, was probably used for ritual ceremonies, but no clues remain to show what actually took place. All that the archaeologist could discover was that the ditches of the cursus had already silted up and become covered with grass before the henge monument was built over them. A similar cursus

visible. Excavations have shown that the bank was originally covered with white gypsum crystals, brought from deposits down the River Ure. Similar circles have been found on Hutton Moor and at Cana, although these are less well preserved and are heavily ploughed down.

The henge monuments in the Ripon area are circular areas surrounded by a bank and ditches. Probably the area inside was sacred land and the bank and ditch were dug to deter the uninitiated from entering the holy ground unbidden. As to the rites which were performed there or what belief they embody, these curious monuments are silent.

The central circle at Thornborough was built over a still earlier structure known as a *Cursus*. This was a ceremonial avenue, running for nearly a mile in a north-east/south-westerly direction. The avenue is defined by ditches 144 feet apart with a bank running along the inside of each ditch. The ditches are now completely filled with plough soil,

Fig. 17 *The Devil's Arrows, near Boroughbridge*

33

runs for over a mile at Scorton, near Catterick in Swaledale.

To this same period probably belongs one of the most famous monuments in Yorkshire, the Devil's Arrows, south-west of Borough-bridge (fig. 17). The Arrows are three natural stones, now heavily weathered into a fluted shape at the top. They stand almost in line along a north to south axis, 200 feet and 370 feet apart. They are massive stones, the largest rising to a height of 22½ feet, and are of millstone grit quarried 6½ miles away to the south-west at Knaresborough. Another,

but single, standing stone now stands in Rudston churchyard some 5¼ miles west of Bridlington. This stone is 25½ feet high and must have been brought over 10 miles to its final resting-place. Clearly their significance must have been great to justify the amount of labour involved in their transportation and erection. The long mounds and round bar-rows, the henge monuments and standing stones show that man was prepared to spend much of his time and energy on work which could give him no direct return in terms of food and shelter.

4 Food Vessels and Collared Urns

Under Beaker stimulus the native potters who had previously been making Peter-borough Ware now began to produce two new forms of pot—the *Food Vessel* and the *Collared Urn*.

Of the two, the food vessel (fig. 18, no. 1) shows the greater Beaker influence. From Beaker traditions are drawn the flat base, the use of a comb with rectangular teeth to make impressed designs, and patterns set out in horizontal zones. The old native tastes survive in the hollow neck and the frequent use of cord to make such patterns as herring-bone. As sometimes happens when members of two distinct traditions exchange and share ideas, the product often shows features which are entirely new, drawn from neither parent. So the hollow neck of the old Peterborough bowl is often doubled and lugs are added to span them.

In contrast the collared urns are less affected by Beaker tastes and continue for some time to use the old patterns most favoured by the potters of Peterborough Ware. The upper part of the urn is covered with incised or cord-impressed herring-bone and the simple form of the Peterborough bowl is retained, though the rim is now deepened into the 'collar' which gives the pot its name (fig. 18, no. 2). The most obvious Beaker contribution is the small flat base, but occa-sionally an urn is decorated in pure Beaker fashion in horizontal zones like the strange vessel (fig. 18, no. 3) found beneath one of the round barrows near Folkton.

Very little is known about the settlements of these food vessel and urn users. Once again it is the burials which provide most of the information. Of the two, the food vessel had the shortest life and was probably

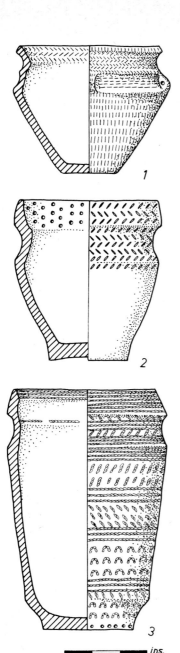

not made in the county after 1300 B.C. The urns continue to be made much later, perhaps until 1000 B.C. before they, too, disappear from the scene.

FOOD VESSELS

Food vessels have been frequently found in northern and eastern England as well as Scotland, Ireland, and Wales. They vary in shape from open bowls to elegant vases and reflect local tastes. In Yorkshire the most common form is the vase, which was probably first developed in north-east England. Not only does the 'Yorkshire Vase' owe much to Beaker influence, but occasionally vase and beaker were found together in the same grave. In fact, many food-vessel burials closely resemble the Beaker burials already described. They are mostly found either beneath round barrows or placed in pits dug into an existing mound. Food vessels are frequently found with crouched skeletons and here probably served the same function as the beaker—a container of food or drink for the dead. Like beakers, they have been found in large numbers on the chalk wolds and on the limestone hills north of the Vale of Pickering. A few have been found on the Howardian Hills and some near the coast at Boulby, for instance, at Hinderwell and Peak. They are rather more frequent than beakers in the West Riding, where they have been found near to the Pennine trade routes at West Tanfield, Ferry Fryston, on Baildon Moor, near Grassington, at Pule Hill near Huddersfield and elsewhere.

Not all food-vessel burials, however, conform to the old Beaker practices. On the limestone hills they are often enclosed in stone cists. Nor were food vessels always placed with inhumations, a number accompany cremated remains. The Quernhow barrow covered several burials of this type.

Fig. 18 *Food vessel: 1 from Bishop Burton; early collared urns, 2 from Ganton, and 3 from Folkton*

QUERNHOW

The Quernhow barrow was excavated in 1949 when the construction of a new carriageway on the Great North Road meant its total destruction. The barrow lay in the Vale of York near Ainderby Quernhow, north of Ripon. Careful excavation showed that the barrow was not a simple structure but had been built in several distinct stages. At the centre a double pit had first been dug apparently for some ceremony, for no burials were made, and then filled up again. Three much smaller hollows were dug nearby and in two of these food vessels were placed. The first burial, a cremation, was accompanied by a third vessel and placed next to the central pit. This area was then covered by a heap of sand and cobbles. Next, the cremated remains of an adult and child were placed at the foot of this heap, and on top were added two further cremations, each with a food vessel. These new burials were then covered with a second mound of sand which covered an area some 20 feet in diameter. The mound was surrounded by a wall of cobbles, but an entrance was left on the east side. A third layer of soil and sand was then thrown over the site, increasing the mound to a height of $2\frac{1}{2}$ feet and the diameter to 50 feet. This mound was finally capped with stones and round its base a ring of large curb stones was added. The total diameter had now become 64 feet.

At a later date the mound was used for further burials. The stone capping was partially removed. A cremation of an adult was buried on the north-west side and the cremated bones of an adult and child, together with a food vessel and flint knife, were buried on the south-west side beneath a small heap of cobbles. The mound was then enlarged to a diameter of 100 feet by heaping more sand over the site. The last burial, another cremation, was placed in a pit dug into this enlarged mound.

Many of the round barrows which can still be seen in the Yorkshire countryside could probably tell a similar story of successive burial and development if carefully excavated. For many, however, the chance has been lost, for the plough has destroyed much of the mound and only the earliest burials will now remain intact.

Perhaps the most striking food-vessel burials are those which have been found in coffins made of oak. Coffin burials of this type have come to light at Old Sunderlandwick, Towthorpe, and Hanging Grimston in the East Riding, at Brotton in the North, near West Tanfield and at Rylstone in the West Riding. But the best-preserved examples are both from the North Riding at Gristhorpe on the coast and Loose Howe high up on the Moors.

THE GRISTHORPE
AND LOOSE HOWE BURIALS

The Gristhorpe burial was found in the central barrow of three on Gristhorpe cliff, between Scarborough and Filey. The coffin, made from the trunk of an oak split in half and hollowed out, was $7\frac{1}{2}$ feet long, 3 feet 3 inches wide at the head, tapering to 2 feet 10 inches at the foot. Its lid was also of oak and had probably been made from the same tree. The coffin and its contents had survived because they lay at the bottom of a pit dug 10 feet into the boulder clay and had become waterlogged. Inside the coffin was the skeleton of a powerfully built man about 6 feet tall lying at full length. The body had been wrapped in an animal skin which had been fastened at the chest by a bone pin. By his side lay his bronze knife with its whalebone pommel, a thin spatula of wood and part of a horn ring. Though the Gristhorpe coffin was square at one end and rounded at the other and looks like a canoe, it may never have been used as a real boat. But in the round barrow at Loose Howe there can be no doubt that an actual canoe had been interred with the coffin containing the primary or earliest burial.

Loose Howe lies far from the sea, high up on the northern moors at a height of 1,400 feet, a few yards north of the road from Ralph Cross to Rosedale Abbey. The barrow was about 7 feet high and 60 feet in diameter. It was excavated by Mr and Mrs Elgee in 1937. They record that when they struck the end of the coffin gallons of water poured out and, as at Gristhorpe, it was this waterlogged state which had led to its preservation. The coffin had once contained a body lying at full length, probably wrapped in linen, though the bones themselves did not survive. The body lay on a bed of rushes and straw and more straw had been added to form a pillow. A piece of shoe and a fragment of foot wrapping still survived and a bronze knife lay beside the left hip. Hazel branches and husks of nuts placed in the coffin show that the burial had been made some time during the autumn.

With the coffin lay a 9-foot-long dugout canoe. The trunk had been hollowed out to a depth of more than a foot and the craft was more than 2 feet wide at the prow. The canoe shows several refinements. The prow had been carved into a projecting beak, and a T-shaped slot cut beneath the stern would have taken a stabilizing board. Along the bottom a keel had been carefully carved, but the bark had been left on the sides to increase the natural buoyancy of the boat.

These burials in which organic material has in part survived give an important glimpse into the lives and appearance of the people. Clearly dugout canoes were being used, at least on the rivers, and probably played an important part in the trade which brought bronze weapons and tools to the Yorkshire communities. Some of these bronze tools, like the gold ornaments of the period which came from Ireland, must have been brought across the Pennines by way of the river valleys which gave relatively easy access through the high moors. Raw materials for any bronzes which were made locally must also have been traded, for Yorkshire has no natural supplies of copper and tin.

The Loose Howe burial shows that shoes were worn and ankles were protected by wrapping strips of cloth round the lower leg like a puttee. The main garment was a buttoned tunic of woven cloth, though its precise shape is still uncertain. Heavier cloaks were probably made out of animal skins. Most men who could afford such things possessed a bronze knife carried in a sheath at the waist. Many, too, must have carried a bronze axe like the young man buried beneath a round barrow near Butterwick.

THE BUTTERWICK GRAVE

The man lay on his left side with his hands in front of his chest at the bottom of a large pit, 10 feet across and 5½ feet deep. In his right hand he still clutched the horn handle of a fine bronze knife, originally carried in a wooden sheath, though only a trace of this survived. Resting on the metal knife was a second made of flint. The new metal implements had by no means ousted the old flint tools even when a man could afford to possess them. Beneath the bronze knife lay a bronze awl once probably set into a wooden or bone handle, though no trace of this remained. In front of the chest lay six V-perforated buttons, five of jet and one of sandstone. They lay where they had fallen from his tunic when it had decayed to dust. Slung from the hips lay an axe once perhaps in a wooden sheath. The blade was of bronze. Its wooden handle could be traced as a dark line of decayed wood extending from the hips towards the heels and was almost 2 feet long. A flint scraper had been tossed into the grave and fragments of a broken food vessel were also recovered.

This Butterwick burial shows that jet was still being used for buttons and indeed the finest necklaces belong to this period. One found at Middleton-on-the-Wolds (fig. 19) is now in Hull Museum. When complete this would have consisted of three to four strings of oblong or disk-shaped beads. The strings were separated and held in position by flat plates, decorated on the outside by a dotted pattern and bored internally to allow threads to pass through.

THE FOLKTON DRUMS
AND CUP-MARKED STONES

The food-vessel users of Yorkshire left behind them more than just their personal belongings. They also left some intriguing problems. What, for example, are the Folkton 'drums'? These drums (fig. 20) are made of chalk and the largest is about 5½ inches across. All three are carefully carved with designs including filled triangles and lozenges which recall pat-terns used on long-necked beakers. But some features do not belong here. The stylized faces and the concentric circles link these curious objects with similar features which occur throughout the Mediterranean, in Spain, Portugal, France, and parts of central and northern Europe. The drums were found in a grave of a 5-year-old child. The smallest was touching the head and the remaining two had been placed near the hips. Were these idols or pretty things for a child's amusement? It is hard to say, but the care with which they had been carved suggests that they were objects of considerable value.

The concentric circles link the Folkton 'drums' to the many stones and rocks in the Yorkshire countryside which are carved with 'cup' and 'ring' marks. These are circular hollows pecked into the rock's surface (fig. 21) sometimes surrounded by concentric rings. They are found over a wide area, but are most common in the West Riding between the Rivers Aire and Nidd. The stones seem to fall into groups with a scatter of more isolated stones around them. One group can be found on Addingham High

Fig. 19 *Jet necklace from Middleton-on-the-Wolds, restored parts in red*

Fig. 20 *One of the Folkton 'drums'*

Moor and Ilkley Moor, a second on Burley Moor and a third on Baildon Moor. A fourth group lies on the Snowden, Askwith, and Weston Moors. More recently Mr Feather has discovered new groups in the mid-Wharfedale area on Middleton Moor and on Rivock, Rombalds Moor, and near Appletreewick to the north.

Occasionally 'cup and ring' marked stones have been found in the same mound as food-vessel burials. Over a hundred and fifty cup-marked stones were found in a barrow heaped over a food-vessel grave at Hinderwell Beacon in the North Riding. Similarly in Howe Hill, Brotton, sixteen cup-marked stones were found in a mound raised over an oak-coffin burial. What these curious carvings were meant to represent we do not know.

COLLARED URNS

The collared urn served two functions. To the living it was a storage vessel; for the dead a last resting-place for the cremated bones. Its users were farmers like those who made and used the food vessels, though farmers who relied more perhaps upon their herds and flocks and less upon agriculture. Yet cereals were grown by these people, for grain impressions are occasionally preserved on the surface of their pots. These impressions show that barley was still being grown as the main crop, at least in the east of the county.

The round barrow remains the characteristic monument of the period, for most collared-urn burials occur as the earliest burial beneath the mound or as later additions to earlier mounds. A few also occur in simple pits dug into the ground without a mound and some occur in more complicated structures. Like food vessels, they are found mainly on the dry soils of the wolds and the limestone hills above the Vale of Pickering. Only a handful have been found in the West Riding, but these are amongst the most interesting, for they are sited along the main trade routes through the Pennine passes. Burials at Halifax and above Todmorden mark the route through the Calder valley. Those on Baildon Moor lie near the route through Airedale; that at Tarnbury near Grassington, the route which passed through Wharfedale.

Although over 400 early collared urns have been found in England and Wales, little is

Fig. 21 *Cup-marked stone on Green Crag Slack, Ilkley Moor*

really known about the lives of these farmers. No true settlements have yet been found in Yorkshire and the burial custom deprives us of much useful information. Cremation destroys the skeleton and these Bronze Age folk with real northern thrift placed few things with their dead. A few beads were occasionally cut from a cherished necklace and sometimes a small personal knife was sacrificed, but little else. Some of these knives have been exposed to intense heat and have warped. No doubt these were still being worn when the body was lifted on to the funeral pyre.

Once the pyre had cooled sufficiently the bones were collected and placed either in an upright urn or heaped together beneath an inverted urn. In the hill country, where stone was readily to hand, the upright urn often had a flat stone placed over its mouth as a lid to keep the soil away from the bones.

On a few occasions a second vessel was inverted over the bones to form a cover. This curious custom was encountered at the site of Blackheath Cross near Todmorden.

BLACKHEATH CROSS

This site was excavated in 1898. It lay on the moorland to the north of Todmorden, at a height of 925 feet. A 'ring cairn' had been built, formed by a circular bank of earth and stones, enclosing an open area about 100 feet across. The cremation burials had all been placed in upright urns. One cremation had been placed in the bank, but the rest lay within the circle. An area of charcoal to the north of the centre probably marked the site of the funeral pyres. The excavators found that, while the bones in the urns were in large fragments and generally unmixed with charcoal, there were also a number of pits containing little or no pottery but a mass of charcoal mixed with fine powdered bone. Clearly when the funeral pyre had cooled the main fragments of bone had been collected first and placed in the urn. The remaining debris from the pyre, which was mainly charcoal, was then carefully placed in a separate pit. The bones had been collected together in a cloth which had been secured with a bone pin. Three of these bone pins were found in the urns.

Two of the burials were exceptional in having several objects placed with them in the urn. With the central burial was a small bronze knife and a bronze awl, bone and clay beads and a small, highly decorated, pottery cup. These small cups (fig. 22, below) are often found with urns, though on some occasions they alone accompany the cremation. They are known to archaeologists by many names: 'pygmy cups', for instance, to emphasize their small size, and 'incense cups', for many have thought that the unpleasant smell made by a funeral pyre would require some sort of fragrant herb to be burnt. The archaeologist has no way to prove or disprove this suggestion.

The other cremation lay within an upright urn and had a second collared vessel inverted inside it as a cover. With the bones lay a pygmy cup and a number of beads, some of jet, some of amber and four of segmented faience. Faience is a form of glass and a man-made substance first invented in the Near East. It was used to make a wide range of objects, but especially beads. Segmented beads (fig. 22, above) were traded to Britain over a relatively short period between 1550 and 1400 B.C.

THE WESSEX CULTURE

Most of these exotic blue beads were traded to the rich communities living in Wessex (the modern counties of Dorset, Somerset, Wiltshire, Hampshire, and Berkshire), which seem to have controlled one of the major trade routes to the west. It was the desire for raw materials, especially the copper and gold of Ireland and the tin of Cornwall, which led the more advanced communities of the eastern Mediterranean to send their traders and prospectors to what to them must well have seemed the ends of the earth. So the Wessex people grew rich on the proceeds of the trade which they controlled and some of this personal

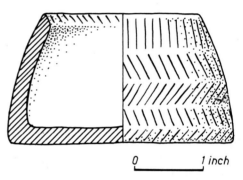

Fig. 22 *Pygmy cup* (*below*) *from Bradford and segmented faience bead* (*above*)

wealth was buried with them when they died. Objects of gold, amber, and faience are far more numerous in these graves than anywhere else in Bronze Age Britain. Superb bronze daggers were made for the Wessex chiefs, some with hilts studded with minute gold nails. Fine bronze dress pins were brought in from Germany. Even the burial mounds are distinctive. For men a bell barrow was often erected, a round barrow with a flat space left between the mound and the ditch, called a *berm*. Women were buried in disc barrows, a monument similar in form to the Todmorden ring cairn, but, being on chalk, made of chalk and earth instead of earth and stone.

EXOTIC IMPORTS IN YORKSHIRE

Outside Wessex these rich burials are rare in southern England. In the north they are still less common, but, occasionally, a few exotic imports reached the area either brought or traded from Wessex, probably in return for jet. In this way the four faience beads which had been made in the east Mediterranean reached the grave near Todmorden. Faience beads were also buried with two collared urns beneath a round barrow on Callis Wold.

The native craftsmen occasionally tried to copy imported dress pins. A copy of a multi-ring-headed pin made of bone was found at Brough (fig. 23, no. 4). Another made of bronze (fig. 23, no. 2) was found with a secondary burial in the Loose Howe barrow, the primary burial of which lay in the oak coffin already described. The cremation lay amongst the fragments of a plain collared urn which had once contained the bronze pin, a fine bronze dagger (fig. 23, no. 3), a stone battle-axe and a pygmy cup. The stone battle-axe (fig. 23, no. 1), of a much more elegant form than those found with the earlier Beaker burials, is also a weapon found with 'Wessex' burials in the south of England. It was probably, like the bronze dagger, a display weapon intended to impress, though still effective if used in anger.

Yorkshire, then, participated to some extent in the wealth which came mainly to Wessex. But in the main the food vessel and early collared urn farmers seem to have lived

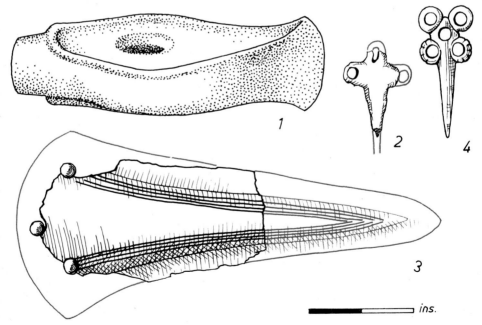

Fig. 23 *Objects found in a secondary grave in Loose Howe: 1 stone battle-axe, 2 bronze pin, and 3 bronze dagger, restored parts in red, 4 bone pin from Brough*

relatively peaceful and uneventful lives. They farmed the drier lands of Yorkshire, obtaining the bronze tools and weapons they needed by trade, and copied the rarer imported trinkets in local jet. Only the problems of a rising population and the need to find new land came to trouble the peace of the Middle Bronze Age.

5 Expansion and Innovation

A PERIOD OF STEADY EXPANSION—THE MIDDLE BRONZE AGE

Though the food vessel passed out of use, the collared urn was still being made down to about 1000 B.C. Naturally over a period of some 600 years the potters developed new tricks of decoration and new ideas of form. It is for this reason that one can tell the difference between the earlier and later urns. If these later burials were to be plotted on a map a significant change would be seen. The population had clearly expanded. While the wolds and the limestone hills were still favoured, the need to find new land had forced some of the farmers to move on to the northern moors and on to the moors of the Pennines in the west.

From about 1400 B.C. marked differences appear between the collared urns produced in the north-west of England and those made in the south-east. For the most part Yorkshire is the meeting-ground of the two styles. Urns decorated with the typical incised patterns of the north-west (fig. 24, above) are found alongside the bipartite forms typical of the south-east (fig. 24, below). In the West Riding, however, the collared urns belong almost entirely to the north-western style which developed over an area stretching from Cumberland in the north to Derbyshire in the south. For once the Pennines formed not so much a barrier as a common homeland which united the hill farmers into a distinct group.

Their way of life is hardly known, for no farmsteads have been excavated. In the West Riding the hill farmers occasionally sheltered in a cave, but they left little behind them. Even their burials are unhelpful, for the custom of placing some personal keepsake with the dead, even if only a bead, soon died out.

RING CAIRNS AND STONE CIRCLES

Many of these late collared-urn burials were placed in pits dug into existing Beaker and food-vessel barrows, especially on the wolds. But on the moors new round barrows were raised over the dead. Stone was available here and many of these moorland barrows have a curb of large stones running round the base of the mound. Other burials lie at the centre of ring cairns like the one on Danby Rigg about 1½ miles south of Danby. Some of these ring cairns contain large standing stones, though at Danby only one of these, some 5 feet high, now survives.

A stone circle 700 yards north-west of Yockenthwaite on the north bank of the River Wharfe is probably another burial site. This circle, about 25 feet across, still contains

43

twenty stones set mostly edge to edge. To the north-west, outside the circle, are four more stones forming part of an outer circle. At the centre a slight mound can be detected and this probably marks the central grave. Not all stone circles are necessarily associated with burials. The remains of one about 30 feet across can be seen near Bradup Bridge in Brass Castle Pasture. Five more can still be seen on Ilkley Moor. Of these the Twelve

Apostles Circle had been set in a bank of earth and stones, 52 feet in diameter. Most of the stones which had once been upright have now fallen. About twenty stones in the Grubstones Circle remain set edge to edge again in a bank of earth, and at least forty-six of the stones in the Horncliffe Circle can still be seen. At this site there are traces of a smaller circle round the centre.

The gradual increase in population was probably due to improved farming methods. Excavations at a settlement at Gwithian in Cornwall have shown that by the beginning of the Middle Bronze Age a simple light scratch plough was already in use in some parts of England, for traces of the actual plough furrows were preserved clearly in the sand. The introduction of the plough would have led to a more systematic production of cereal crops in regular fields. A larger population could then have been supported. The farmers, too, were by now equipped with a better form of bronze axe.

BRONZE IMPLEMENTS AND POPULATION DRIFT

The bronze industries had made progress, though metal implements were still not common and the range of tools made was limited. Improved techniques included the use of moulds of two or more components. The new form of axe, the palstave, was made in a composite type of mould which allowed a stop-ridge and side flanges to be cast. The stop-ridge prevented the axe being pushed back and so splitting the haft while the flanges made the hafting more rigid (fig. 25a, right). The principal weapons were the socketed spearhead (fig. 25a, left), often provided with side loops on the socket so that the head could be bound firmly to the wooden shaft, and the rapier. The rapier (fig. 25b) is a thrusting sword with sharp point and narrow blade. Only three have been found

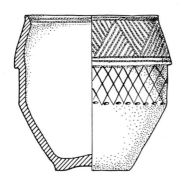

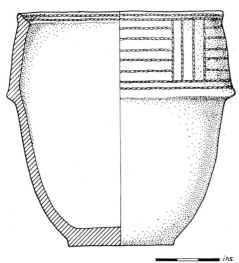

ins.

Fig. 24 *Late collared urns from Warley (above) and Crosscliff (below)*

44

in Yorkshire, at Cayton near Scarborough, Misson and Flotmanby near Filey. These farmers seem to have been peaceable folk, but if the need arose they were quite capable of defending themselves, and a growing population with the need to find new land probably led to some fighting. Though much of the best land had by now been occupied, there was still room for expansion on to poorer ground and the more adventurous left the county altogether. Scotland was colonized by collared-urn users at this time, and the main wave of colonists entering eastern Scotland made pottery very like the urns found on the northern moors. A few of these colonists perhaps returned with wives or friends, for three burials in eastern Yorkshire were made in cordoned urns, a type which had developed independently in Scotland. So close is the likeness of the cordoned urn found beneath one of the round barrows on Garrowby Wold with vessels in Aberdeenshire that it can be safely assumed the potter came from that part of north-east Scotland.

CROWN END

A number of possible settlement sites in the North Riding may belong to the end of the Middle Bronze Age, though without extensive excavation it is difficult to pick out features which can be definitely assigned to this period rather than to the Iron Age. So far excavations have been small and inconclusive. A typical site of this type lies on a spur called Crown End, about 1½ miles south-west of Castleton in upper Eskdale. The spur is about two-thirds of a mile wide and rises to a height of over 750 feet.

The settlement includes a circular embanked enclosure 129 feet across with standing stones set into its walls. Field walls and cleared plots can be made out, and the various pits and hollows are evidence of occupation.

A large number of small cairns of stone, 6–12 feet across, can also be seen on the spur. These suggest a cemetery of burial mounds, yet when this type of cairn has been opened

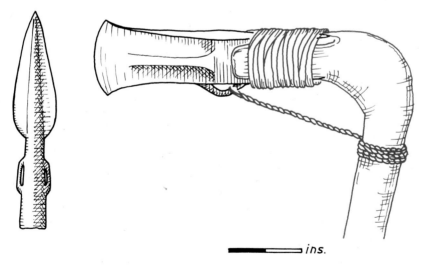

ins.

Fig. 25a *Socketed spearhead from Bowes and; palstave from Thornton le Clay, hafting restored in red*

45

both here and on Kildare Moor few traces of burial have been found. Possibly some were heaped over inhumations which have rotted without trace, but so far this has not been proved. Their date is still uncertain.

THE PROBLEM OF THE LATE BRONZE AGE

By about 1000 B.C. the practice of burying the dead in collared urns had virtually died out. Between this date and the arrival of new immigrants from the Continent the prehistory of Yorkshire poses many problems. No satisfactory settlements have yet been found and only a handful of cremation burials in plain, bucket-shaped pots seem to date from this phase. Yet there is abundant evidence in the shape of stray finds and hoards of bronze implements that the population of Yorkshire in the Late Bronze Age was by no means small.

Late Bronze Age finds frequently occur in the lowlands and river valleys, in sharp contrast to the upland concentration of sites in the preceding periods. Many objects have been found in the south-east of the county in the low-lying plain of Holderness and again along the northern fringe of the Vale of Pickering. In the West Riding finds tend to be concentrated between Tadcaster in the Vale of York and Leeds, and again farther up the Vale between Ripon and Masham. A few implements have also been picked up in the Pennine valleys—in Wensleydale, Airedale, and the Don valley. Though we are dealing here with bronze implements, not burial sites, the move from wold and moor to plain and river valley is none the less striking and must surely indicate some shift in population on to lower ground.

DEVELOPMENTS
IN THE BRONZE INDUSTRIES

The Late Bronze Age sees a marked increase in the number of bronze tools now available.

⬛▬▭ ins.

Fig. 25b *Bronze rapier*

Implements like the axe were now mass-produced and the bronzesmith saved metal when he could by hollow-casting. The new standard form of axe was socketed, made in a two-piece mould, with a sand and clay core secured between the two halves (fig. 26, no. 6). When the metal was poured into the top of the mould the bronze could then flow evenly round the core. The mould was then opened, the core removed and a hollow 'socketed' axe produced. Like the socketed spearhead, the socketed axe required a haft which passed inside the socket. A forked branch was first selected. One arm was left long for the handle, the other was trimmed to a stub to fit into the socket. As an additional safeguard the axe was given a small side loop and when hafted this pointed downwards. Thongs were then passed through the loop and bound round the wooden handle (fig. 26, no. 7). This ensured that when in use the axe would not break so easily at the joint through a mistimed blow. Some idea of the scale on which these socketed axes were made and traded can be gathered from the *founders' hoards*.

A founder's hoard really represents the stock-in-trade of a bronzesmith who, probably in fear of being robbed, hid his goods and tools by burying them in the ground. The hoards tell rather a sad tale. Either the smith forgot where he had buried his wealth or his fears of being attacked had been only too well founded. The average Late Bronze Age hoard of this type contains large quantities of scrap metal as well as the personal tool kit of the smith himself. These hoards show how well organized the bronze industry had now become. Not only were finished implements made and traded, but old and broken implements were collected and melted down ready for making into a fresh set of tools. The vast increase in bronze implements during this period was largely due to this re-use of old metal which provided a useful supplementary

source of bronze. The smith also began to add lead as well as tin to the copper, which helped to increase the quantity, though not the quality, of the metal available.

The size of some of these hoards is quite staggering. One found recently by the plough at Isleham in Cambridgeshire contained over 6,500 pieces of bronze, together weighing no less than 200 lb. Yorkshire cannot yet boast of a hoard as large as this, though at least one old find must have come near to it. A hoard

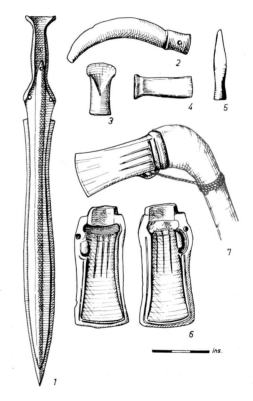

Fig. 26 *Late Bronze Age implements:* 1 *Leaf shaped sword from Brompton,* 2 *socketed sickle,* 3 *socketed gouge,* 4 *socketed hammer,* 5 *socketed chisel,* 6 *mould for socketed axe, and* 7 *socketed axe, from Roseberry Topping, hafting restored in red*

47

found on Yearsley Common on the Howardian Hills near Easingwold is said to have contained more than a hundred axes, together with pieces of melted-down bronze 'cake'.

Besides the socketed axe two other forms of axe were in use during the period. The palstave, despite its uneconomical use of metal, survived for some time and the winged axe was introduced. This was cast solid like the palstave, but the side flanges were exaggerated and bent over so that they almost met.

As metal became more abundant a whole range of specialized tools were developed. The bronzesmith now had, besides his bronze moulds, a bronze anvil, socketed hammers, chisels and gouges (fig. 26, nos. 3–5). As well as axes and knives the farmer had bronze sickles, like that found in a hoard on Roseberry Topping (fig. 26, no. 2). For fighting there was the leaf-shaped sword (fig. 26, no. 1), the blade being now shaped to slash rather than thrust. To parry the blow of the sword a shield was carried. This was usually made of wood or leather, but for display fine, decorated, bronze shields were produced. There was also a choice of socketed spearheads. The heavier ones, mounted on long shafts, would have been used as thrusting weapons; but lighter ones served as javelin heads for throwing. A few could also afford bronze cauldrons, made of sheets of bronze riveted together and provided with a pair of large ring handles so that they could be hung up.

FARMS IN SOUTHERN ENGLAND

For some idea of how these Late Bronze Age farmers are likely to have lived in Yorkshire we must look again outside the county. In southern England regular farmsteads have been excavated showing that the farmers built round timber huts. One such farm, on Itford Hill in Sussex, lay on the southern slopes of the chalk downs not all that dissimilar to the wolds of the East Riding. The farm was large enough to accommodate a single large family and was occupied for perhaps a single generation. In all, thirteen round huts were found each standing on a circular platform cut into the sloping chalk of the hill-side. The chalk scooped out in making the platforms was used to build banks round the huts, to which a light fencing was added. Four of the huts were used as dwellings, the largest being 22 feet across, and each had a porch. Two huts were set aside for storage and in one of these a large quantity of burnt barley grains were found. The remaining huts were probably used for a variety of purposes, including sheltering the cattle during the worst of the winter weather.

In the south of England the farmers were still cremating their dead. Their large flat cemeteries of urn burials imply larger communities living either in groups of farmsteads or even perhaps in small villages. In Yorkshire the cemeteries, like the farms, have still to be found, but the hoards and stray finds of bronze implements are a reminder that these gaps in our knowledge still exist.

6 The Coming of Iron

Despite the gradual expansion of population and the consequent need to find new land, the Bronze Age had been a generally peaceful period in England. Not so on the Continent. By the Late Bronze Age much of central and western Europe was in a state of unrest. The related groups of people, whose large cremation cemeteries have caused them to be known as the Urnfield Culture, were spreading westwards, gradually pushing the earlier inhabitants before them. In their wake came the first iron-using communities of the Hallstatt Culture. By 700 B.C. these first iron-users were spreading out of southern Germany and into eastern France. Before 600 B.C. typical Hallstatt objects were reaching Britain. The majority of these were of bronze, but some were already of iron. A large hoard of bronze implements found at Llyn Fawr in Glamorgan included an iron spearhead, iron sickle, and an iron sword of Hallstatt type.

CASTLE HILL, SCARBOROUGH

By 550 B.C. new immigrants were beginning to arrive in small groups along the eastern and southern shores of England. One such group made landfall on the Yorkshire coast at Scarborough.

About thirty pits were found and excavated beneath the Roman signal station at the eastern end of Castle Hill, Scarborough. The site had clearly been chosen for its defensive qualities —an important consideration for strangers who arrive to colonize a country already inhabited by a population armed with swords and spears. The pits were found to be full of typical domestic rubbish, including sherds of broken pots and bones of domesticated animals. All trace of actual huts had disappeared, but the pits are sufficient to show that this was no temporary camp. They are of a type dug for storing grain and were probably once lined with basketry. Even so, after only a short while, this type of pit becomes sour and unsuitable for storage purposes; they were then used as rubbish dumps. Though the site belongs to the beginning of the Iron Age the only piece of iron actually found was a small fragment from an iron pin. Many of the sherds found in the pits belong to large bucket-shaped pots with flat bases. Several have a strip of clay or 'cordon' applied to the surface a little way below the rim (fig. 27, below), and this is often decorated with a row of finger-tip impressions or a row of slashes. More shapely vessels with concave necks and outward flaring rims were also made (fig. 27, above).

Similar pottery has been found on a number of sites, most of which lie in eastern Yorkshire—at Thornholm Hill, for example, in Holderness, Sledmere, Kendale, and Helperthorpe. But the immigrants did in time penetrate farther into the county. One group settled for a time at Grafton, 3 miles southeast of Boroughbridge. Unfortunately most of this site had been destroyed by a quarry, but a burnt layer in the area examined produced sherds of domestic pottery with bones of ox, horse, pig, and sheep or goat. A hearth was found at one point, but no huts. Two stone-packed trenches which had once probably formed the footings for timber walls were found, but due to the quarry, neither

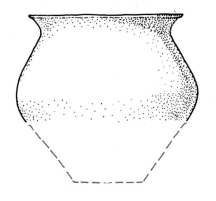

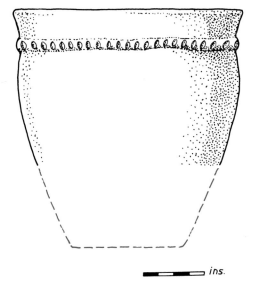

ins.

Fig. 27 *Early Iron Age pottery from Scarborough, bases restored in red*

the extent nor the purpose of these walls could be discovered. Only two fragments of metal were recovered and both of these were bronze. One was a pair of bronze tweezers; the other a fragment of bronze armlet. Fortunately a much clearer picture of the times has been obtained by the complete excavation of a farmstead in the East Riding.

THE STAPLE HOWE FARMSTEAD

Staple Howe is a natural hill of chalk in Knapton Wood on the northern slopes of the wolds, south of the Vale of Pickering. The hill is about 85 feet high and is flat topped, offering a natural platform 180 feet long and 40 feet wide. With a small spring only 300 yards to the east, the hill provided an excellent defensive site. Through T. C. M. Brewster's excavations we can follow the history of a farmstead built on top of this hill.

At an early stage a light timber palisade was set up round the top. This added to the defensive character of the site and at the same time helped to contain the farm animals. At first the palisade enclosed a single oval hut 30 feet long and 20 feet across, set on a platform dug into the chalk. Its walls were made of stone or chalk and the roof must have been gabled, for there was once a row of posts down the centre of the hut. Inside were the remains of a clay oven and a hearth. Over the floor a layer of domestic rubbish had accumulated, including ox bones split so that the marrow could be extracted.

At a later stage this first hut was abandoned and two round huts and a granary took its place. These later huts had been built in a different style. The one at the western end of the settlement had a diameter of 30 feet and the framework of the hut had been made of stout timbers. Though these did not survive, the holes which had been made for the uprights did and so the plan of the framework was permanently recorded. The hut had a central post and a circle of posts marked the outer wall. On the south-east side was a porch. The timbers used in a hut of this type would rot after a few years and would then have to be replaced. The fact that there had been no major replacement of the upright timbers shows clearly that this hut had been used for only a short period. Inside the hut was a hearth and a clay oven. The hut also contained an upright loom whose timber uprights were set $5\frac{1}{2}$ feet apart. This together with the clay loomweights and spindle whorls found during the excavations shows that cloth was woven on the site.

The other hut was similar but slightly smaller and lay at the eastern end of the hill-top. This was less well preserved, but its general circular plan could be made out with a porch again on the south-east side.

In the centre of the farm, on one of the highest points, a small granary had been built. All that remained was the plan of the main timber uprights—five posts forming an 8-foot square. The posts had been massive, 14 inches across and deeply set, but clearly the ground plan was too small for a house. It suggests rather a platform construction. The third post on the east side of the square shows that the roof was gabled, a sloping roof being essential in the wet British climate to drain away the rainwater. Unlike the Scarborough site, no

grain-storage pits were found at Staple Howe, so that the grain must have been stored in a different way. A hut raised above ground-level would have kept the seed grain dry and well away from the animals within the farm enclosure. Considerable quantities of burnt grain were found on the site and a Carbon 14 test on a sample of this gave a date of 440 ± 150 B.C. Figure 28 gives an impression of how the farm would have looked in this final stage.

The animal bones recovered during the excavations show that the farmers kept cattle, goats, sheep, and pigs; they also cultivated wheat. The wild animals of the area are represented by bones of fox, wolf, wild cat, beaver, and badger, as well as both red and roe deer. The farmers of Staple Howe also did some fishing, for bone *gorges* were found on the site. The gorges (fig. 29, no. 3) are small pieces of bone about 2 inches long and pointed at both ends. They were concealed in the bait and when swallowed stuck across

Fig. 28 *The Staple Howe farm in its final phase (after Brewster)*

the fish's throat. Only two objects of iron were found; a fragment of a pin and an iron ring. Bronze objects were more numerous and included two small razors and part of a third. There was also a pair of tweezers, a chisel, two awls, and a fragment of socketed axe. The bronze razors (fig. 29, nos. 1–2) are particularly important, for two were undoubtedly imported from the Continent, probably from Holland. There they date to before 500 B.C.

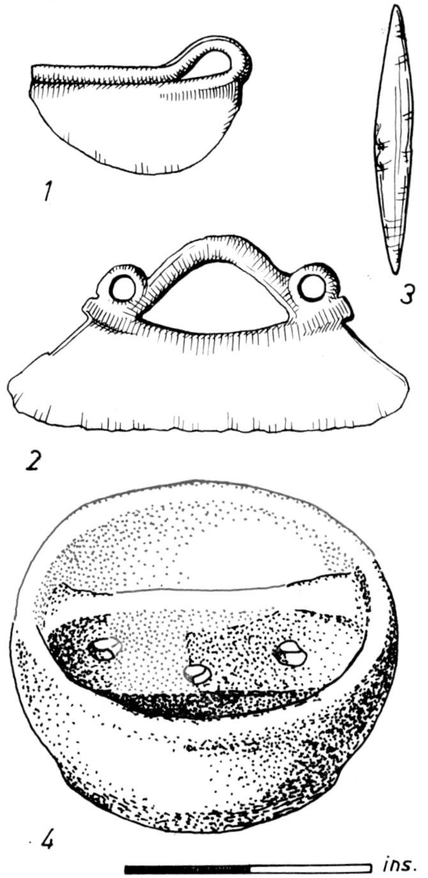

Fig. 29 *Objects found at Staple Howe: 1 and 2 Bronze razors, 3 bone gorge, 4 pottery lamp, restored parts in red*

Armlets, beads, and pendants show that local supplies of jet were still being exploited. Bone was used for pins and netting-needles as well as gorges. Antler picks were still being used, but it is noticeable that only six flints were found on the site. The use of stone implements was at last dying out.

Amongst the large quantities of pottery recovered from the farm were both coarse and fine wares. Bowls and jars were common and also large cooking and storage pots. Finger-tip decoration was frequently used and a few of the late pots have cordon decoration. Pottery lamps (fig. 29, no. 4) show how the huts were lit in the dark areas away from the fire.

THE ARRIVAL OF THE LA TÈNE LORDS

It was not long before new immigrants began to arrive in eastern Yorkshire. They came from France, probably from the region between Paris and Burgundy, and they are known in Yorkshire mainly from their graves.

One of their main cemeteries lay at Arras, now split by the road from Market Weighton to Beverley. Though the plough has almost completely levelled the site, at one time over a hundred round barrows could be seen clustered together. They were all small mounds, between 8 and 30 feet across and at most no more than 3 feet high. Each barrow covered a single body, usually contracted, and placed in a pit dug into the underlying chalk. At least three of the barrows lay within square inclosures, between 34 and 40 feet across, formed by a wide shallow ditch 6 to 8 feet wide and 3 feet deep. This feature is particularly important, for, as I. M. Stead has pointed out, enclosures of this type are not found in the British Isles outside Yorkshire and are rare on the Continent. The fact that they occur in Champagne, especially in the region south of the Marne, helps to establish the homeland of these new-comers.

THE ARRAS CEMETERY

The majority of the graves in the Arras cemetery are simple inhumations accompanied by a few personal ornaments—usually a brooch, a bronze armlet, rings or beads. For some reason no weapons or pottery were buried with the dead. One rich lady had been buried wearing a necklace of almost a hundred blue and white glass beads. An amber ring lay in front of her as well as the bronze brooch which secured her dress and a bronze pendant, both decorated with white coral. Nearby lay her bronze armlets, two small bronze rings, a bronze pin, a gold finger ring, and a pair of bronze tweezers. Set against the other graves in the cemetery, this woman was clearly something more than just a commoner.

Three other graves in the cemetery stand quite apart from the rest. In one lay the skeleton of a woman, aged between 35 and 40, lying on her left side with her left hand in front of her face. Behind her head lay the bones of two pigs and beneath them had been placed her iron mirror. Around her lay the dismantled remains of a chariot. The two wheels had been placed behind her back though only the iron tyres and the bronze nave bands which went round the central part of the wheel remained. The diameter of the tyres shows that the wheels were originally 34 inches across. In front of her face lay two bridle bits of iron coated with bronze, which show that the chariot had been pulled by two horses. An iron and bronze ring, also found in the grave, would have belonged to the harness which had been thrown in with the burial. Here was a woman of noble birth interred in her chariot, which on her death had been used as a funeral cart to carry the body to the grave.

In the 'King's Barrow' a second chariot lay dismantled round the extended skeleton of an old man. In this grave the two horses had also been interred with their master. In a third grave the bronze boss of a shield was found along with a two-wheeled chariot, but no offensive weapons.

These graves in the Arras cemetery show that the latest immigrants were led by men (and perhaps women, too), of noble birth, who in war were accustomed to fight from chariots drawn by pairs of horses surrounded by their followers on foot. A similar distinction between 'noble' and 'commoner' was found in a second large cemetery, the Danes' Graves, 4 miles north of Driffield.

THE DANES' GRAVES CEMETERY

Estimates of the exact size of the original Danes' Graves cemetery vary, but at one time there were probably about 500 small round barrows of the type found at Arras. The people buried in the Danes' Graves seem to have been less rich than their Arras cousins and those who buried their dead in a similar but smaller cemetery at Cowlam. In many graves no offerings were found, in others just a small flat-based pot, undecorated and carelessly finished. Yet if personal belongings could only rarely be spared at least the dead were not to go hungry. Four of the pots were found to contain the remains of a leg of pork and a whole pig had been placed in one of the graves.

A few graves contained personal ornaments. These were mainly the iron brooches which had fastened the garments of the dead, but two fine bronze brooches (fig. 30, below) were also recovered. On the Continent, where the type developed, these brooches were made on the safety-pin principle, having a coiled spring at one end while the point fitted into a catch plate at the other. These two bronze brooches, however, were made in Britain, for they show the curious British trick of imitating the coils of the spring, but in fact hooking the end of the pin round a simple pivot passing through the coils. This is hardly a technical improvement and is a sad reflection on the skill of the local craftsmen. One of the brooches was decorated on the bow, and a fine wheel-headed bronze pin (fig. 30, above) from the cemetery was decorated with studs made from Mediterranean coral. From the

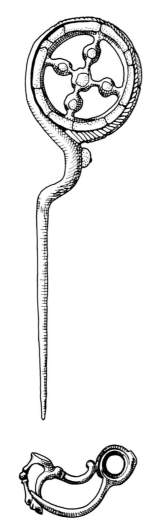

Fig. 30 *Bronze wheel-headed pin (above) and bronze brooch (below) from Danes' Graves*

entire cemetery the only other ornaments to be found were four metal armlets, two being of bronze and two of iron, part of a jet bracelet and some beads.

In contrast to these simple graves, a large grave, 9 feet long and 7½ feet wide, contained the contracted skeletons of two men and the dismantled remains of another two-wheeled chariot. Half a pig had also been placed in the grave.

OTHER CHARIOT BURIALS

Chariot burials are not confined to these two cemeteries. Others have been found on the Wolds at Hunmanby, at Westwood near Beverley, and probably, but less certainly, at Haywold near Huggate and Enthorpe. In the North Riding they have been found at Seamer, Pexton Moor, and at Cawthorn Camps. The chariot burial at Cawthorn, unlike the ones at Arras and Danes' Graves, was placed in the grave complete and not dismantled. The decayed woodwork showed clearly in the sand of the barrow which had been heaped over it. The two wheels with their iron tyres were four spoked and almost 3 feet across. The nave bands were made of iron plated with bronze. Even the chariot pole could be traced out as a line of decayed wood some 7 feet beyond the body of the chariot.

It is a curious fact that these pig-eating Frenchmen buried no weapons with their dead either at Arras or Danes' Graves or in any of the chariot graves. Yet iron weapons were certainly in use in the county by this time. The fighting kit of the period was probably that of the warrior interred at Grimthorpe near Pocklington. With him in the grave were his two-edged iron sword, an iron spearhead, the remains of a shield decorated with bronze fittings and some bone spear points. For those who could afford the luxury, the bronze craftsmen were soon turn-

Fig. 31 *The Bugthorpe scabbard*

ing out superb bronze sword sheaths. One of these was found at Bugthorpe (fig. 31). The finely engraved hatched tendril design is a good example of the insular form of La Tène art.

THE LA TÈNE STYLE OF ART

The La Tène art style developed on the Continent largely under the patronage of the aristocratic chieftains of the period who had the wealth and prestige to attract craftsmen to work for them. In Britain the La Tène craftsmen developed their own insular style in which palmettes, tendrils, and scrolls are particularly prominent. This art found its finest expression in the decoration of a series of bronze mirror backs and hence has come to be known as the 'mirror style'. The incised and hatched patterns of the mirror style were also occasionally used on objects of display and the Bugthorpe scabbard is an early example of its use on weapons.

With the Bugthorpe sword were two bronze disks to which were riveted studs of red enamel. These undoubtedly imitate coral studs like those used on the wheel-headed pin from the Danes' Graves cemetery. Soon enamel was being used in the *champlevé* technique to cover larger areas of surface. In this method, a pattern was created by casting a socket for the enamel in the surface of the metal. This socket was then filled with enamel, fused into position, until the surface was level with that of the surrounding metal. A fine three-piece bridle bit, found at Rise near Hull in Holderness, is decorated in this way with blue and red enamel inlays (fig. 32). Horse-trappings were frequently decorated, and many of the objects in the large Stanwick hoard were originally decorated with small spots of coloured enamel.

THE STANWICK HOARD

A large hoard composed mainly of bronze horse-trappings was found sometime before

55

1845 near Stanwick St John. Historically this hoard is particularly interesting, for when Lord Prudhoe offered the hoard to the British Museum he did so on condition that a room was provided to house 'national antiquities'. It was the Stanwick hoard, in fact, which formed the nucleus of the British Museum's prehistoric collection.

Fig. 32 *Bronze bit with enamel decoration from Rise*

The hoard consists of a vast array of horse-bits, terrets, harness mounts and lynch pins as well as other oddments. These include the remains of an iron spearhead and a fine 'Brigantian' iron sword in a bronze sheath (fig. 33) like others found at Cotterdale, Flasby, and Thorpe near Bridlington. Many of the objects are broken or damaged and several have bad casting flaws. The hoard seems to have been a founder's hoard comparable to those deposited many centuries earlier in the Late Bronze Age. Amongst the most pleasing objects are two sheet-metal mounts giving the impression of human faces, and a third in the shape of a horse's head (fig. 34). This has been produced by opposing two trumpet scrolls and adding lozenge-shaped eyes. It shows the simple perfection which could now be attained by the bronze craftsmen. Like the Late Bronze Age hoards, the Stanwick hoard was deliberately hidden

during a period of very real unrest, about the middle of the first century A.D.

HILL-FORTS

Intertribal fighting was a common enough occurrence amongst the Iron Age tribes. During the last few centuries B.C. and the

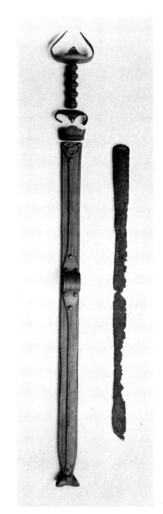

Fig. 33 *Brigantian sword from the Stanwick hoard*

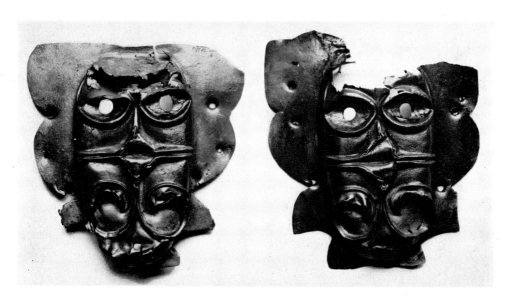

Fig. 34 *Bronze masks from the Stanwick hoard*

first century A.D., hill-forts were built in western and northern Yorkshire. Many of these, like Boltby Scar, Roulston Scar, Castleton Rigg, and Eston Nab, are built on promontories where a natural defensive site has been completed with a man-made rampart and ditch. At Boltby Scar, on the Hambleton Hills, a vertical cliff face forms the western side of the fort, while the accessible side is blocked by a bank and ditch enclosing an area of about 2½ acres. The massive Danes Dyke, north-east of Bridlington, is a far more ambitious affair. This cuts off a peninsula 5 miles square and extends from coast to coast. The bank is 18 feet high; the ditch is 60 feet wide and there are traces of a second bank outside the ditch.

South-east of Huddersfield, the hill-fort at Almondbury encloses something like 16 acres, though its beginnings were considerably smaller. The fort first enclosed only part of the summit plateau. This was then extended, probably in the third century B.C., to enclose the whole plateau within a defensive system of double bank and ditch. Later the inner bank was rebuilt on a timber frame. Finally, about the end of the first century B.C., the area enclosed by the fort was doubled by adding a pair of banks and ditches some way down the hill with an inturned entrance at the western end. If an assault was made on the gate, the attackers would find themselves in a narrow space and in cross-fire from the defenders manning the ramparts on either side.

Many of these hill forts were not inhabited for any length of time. They were refuges for the inhabitants of the nearby valleys in times of tribal strife. Strife there was and until the Roman invasion, the tribes had no common foe to bind them. Even when the Roman army did reach Britain the tribes adopted no common plan. Some sought safety by coming to terms with the invaders, others put a higher price on freedom. By the middle of the first century A.D., hill-forts, Romans, and tribesmen all become part of the same picture. To appreciate this we must now turn to the Roman occupation and the fortifications at Stanwick.

7 *The Roman Occupation*

THE INVASION

The Roman army had invaded Britain in A.D. 43 under an experienced commander, Aulus Plautius. By A.D. 48 the second Governor of Britain, Ostorius Scapula, had carried the invasion as far as the Midlands, and the chief resistance to Roman occupation now centred on the *Brigantes* of the North of England and the tribes of Wales. According to the Roman historian Tacitus, *Brigantia* was 'said to be the most populous state in the whole province'. It certainly stretched from south Yorkshire to Co. Durham, and a dedication to the goddess Brigantia found in a fort at Birrens in Dumfriesshire suggests that the Brigantes may even have stretched as far as southern Scotland. The Roman geographer Ptolemy, writing in the second century A.D., states simply that the Brigantes stretched from sea to sea, but it would probably be nearer the truth to see a loose federation of tribes under the dominance of the Brigantes covering the whole of northern England. The other tribes in the federation were the *Setantii* of western Lancashire, and perhaps the *Textoverdi*, a tribe living in the north-east about which little is at present known. On its borders lay the *Parisi* of eastern Yorkshire.

Ostorius Scapula seems to have come to an understanding with the Brigantes before setting out to crush the resistance in Wales. The Silures of south-east Wales were led by Caratacus, son of Cunobelin of Colchester, who had joined the Silures after the Roman occupation of south-east England. In A.D. 51 Ostorius finally met and defeated Caratacus in a battle somewhere near the Welsh border. Caratacus himself escaped and fled to the Brigantes, but found no welcome. Their queen, Cartimandua, put him in chains and handed him over to the Roman Governor.

This action seems to have led immediately to civil war in the Brigantian federation. The anti-Roman party was led by Venutius, Cartimandua's husband, and he would probably have defeated the pro-Roman party under the queen if the Romans had not come to her aid. An uneasy peace followed, only to be shattered in A.D. 69 when the queen renounced Venutius as her husband and took as her consort his armour-bearer, Vellocatus. This outrageous act at once plunged the Brigantes into further civil war. Cartimandua was again forced to seek Roman help and with some difficulty the Roman troops managed to remove the queen to safety. From this point she disappears from the scene, leaving Venutius as undisputed leader

of the Brigantes and an embittered opponent of Roman rule. It is against this background that Sir Mortimer Wheeler has set his excavations at the Stanwick fortifications.

THE STANWICK FORTIFICATIONS

The fortifications (fig. 35) lie on a rolling piece of land between the modern villages of Aldburgh St John and Caldwell. The site was hardly chosen for its commanding position, for the ground here does not rise above

Fig. 35 *Plan of the Stanwick fortifications showing its three main phases of development (after Wheeler). Phase 2 shown in red*

100 feet. Rather it was chosen as being near a good supply of water, the Mary Wild Beck. In their final form, discounting a later addition on the south side, the earthworks enclosed an area of over 700 acres, but the first fortification was a more modest affair enclosing 17. This more or less coincides with a rough field known as 'the Tofts' south-west of Stanwick church. The defences were impressive, for a man standing on the bottom of the single ditch would look up to a rampart rising to a height of 24 feet. Naturally access had to be provided across the rampart and a gateway was left at the western angle. To strengthen this

point the flanks of the gateway were revetted with dry-stone walling.

Although only a small portion of the area was examined, a series of drainage ditches were found inside the enclosure together with the remains of a round timber hut with an entrance facing east. This was set within a circular drainage ditch, which would have taken the water dripping from the conical roof. An interesting feature which emerged from the excavations at Stanwick was that only a quarter of the pottery recovered was home-made and these were mainly rough cooking-pots. The remainder of the pottery had all been imported. These imported wares included *Butt Beakers* (fig. 36, above) from south-east England and fine red *Samian Ware* (fig. 36, below) made towards the end of the first century A.D. in Gaul. The builders of the fortifications then had wide trading contacts with other tribes living farther south. This first fortification was probably built as a centre for anti-Roman resistance in northern Brigantia, shortly after the Roman invasion of A.D. 43.

At a later date the fortifications were greatly enlarged (see fig. 35). An enclosure of 130 acres was built to the north to supplement the first fortifications. This new enclosure cut off the northern end of the earlier work and, where this lay within the new enclosure, the old ramparts were flattened. The new enclosure was deliberately built to include some 300 yards of the Mary Wild Beck and, along this stretch, the brook and its marshy borders formed the only defence. Towards the western angle the new rampart was side-stepped to provide an entrance. This new rampart, which had originally been marked out with a small bank and ditch, was revetted in front by vertical dry-stone walling to a height of about 15 feet. Between the rampart and the ditch lay a *berm*—a flat space about 1 foot wide. The vertical height

from the bottom of the ditch to the top of the rampart when first erected must have been something like 28 feet (fig. 37).

Near the entrance a pool of muddy water had collected in the bottom of the ditch. This had helped to preserve the organic objects that had either fallen or been thrown in. An oak dish was found and fragments of basketry, as well as an iron sword in a bronze-

Fig. 36 *Butt beaker and Samian bowl from Stanwick (after Wheeler), restored parts in red*

bound scabbard made of ash wood (fig. 38). Near the sword lay a skull showing very definite signs that its owner had met with a violent death. The skull had been slashed twice across the eye and a third blow had sliced off a piece of frontal bone which lay nearby. The head had been severed from the body between the fourth and fifth vertebrae. The victim was perhaps a criminal or prisoner and may well have suffered the fate of having his head stuck on a pole at the gate.

The final stage of the construction was marked by a huge extension to the enclosure with a bank-berm-and-ditch defensive system similar to the previous fortification (*see* fig. 35).

The new fortifications enclosed some 600 acres and provided ample pasturage for horses and cattle. The entrance lay in the middle of the south rampart in the form of a Z-shaped breach, but no gates were found. This final reconstruction was never completed. The causeway across the ditch opposite the gate had been roughly hacked through and blocks lay where they had been hurriedly levered up. The occupants had clearly had no time to finish their work before being called upon to defend themselves.

It was probably Venutius who extended the fortifications at Stanwick and then extended them again in and after A.D. 69 when

Fig. 37 *The restored rampart and ditch at Stanwick*

61

he was gathering his allies for a final stand against the Romans. The unfinished state of the last phase of the defences shows that the final battle came before the Brigantes were completely ready, and the deliberate destruction of part of the ramparts shows only too clearly the ultimate result of the conflict. The actual struggle is not documented by the historians, but the Roman victory must have been complete, for by A.D. 80 Agricola was campaigning in Scotland. A Scottish campaign would have been out of the question if the Brigantes were still menacing the supply routes to the south.

ROMAN ROADS

The success of the Roman occupation of Britain was largely due to the network of roads and forts which were built throughout the country. In the North of England the majority of these were probably built under Agricola, but the first basic network in the north may well have been established somewhat earlier.

Taking the North of England as a whole, two major arterial roads were constructed— one on either side of the Pennines (fig. 39). In the west the road ran from Chester, which had in A.D. 78 become a legionary fortress, first north-eastwards to Manchester, then northwards to Ribchester, Overborough, Low Barrow Bridge, over Crosby Ravensworth Fell in Westmorland to Brougham, and so to Carlisle. In the east a similar road, starting from either Lincoln and passing through Doncaster and Tadcaster, or from York, then ran north-westwards to Aldborough and Catterick and so to Scotch Corner. Here the road forks. The western branch went north-west through Brough-under-Stainmore to link up with the main western road at Brougham. The eastern branch went almost due north, through Binchester and Ebchester, to Corbridge.

The system was consolidated by a series of roads crossing the country from east to west. Many of these used the Pennine passes which were already well-established routes in the prehistoric period. One road ran from Manchester through Castleshaw and Slack to the Calder Valley, and then linked up with

Fig. 38 *Bronze bound wooden scabbard from Stanwick*

the main east road at Castleford. One of the main routes ran from the fort of Ribchester, through Elslack and Ilkley, to Tadcaster. Another ran from Overborough via Brough-by-Bainbridge into Wensleydale. To the north the western arm of the east road linked Catterick and Brougham via Stainmore. The East Riding was served by a network of roads linking York with Malton and Brough-on-Humber. Wade's Causeway served the North. This began at Amotherby (north-west of Malton) and ran north-north-east across the Vale of Pickering to Cawthorn, then over the moors to Lease Rigg and Eskdale. Beyond the Esk the road cannot be traced, but it probably led to some point on the coast, perhaps Whitby.

By building forts along the roads, the supply routes could be kept open, and help could be brought quickly to any trouble spots which might arise. By placing forts, for example, at Ilkley and Elslack, Agricola kept firm control of the main east to west route through the Aire valley. But the key site for the control of Yorkshire was York itself.

EBURACUM

York, or to give it its Roman name, Eburacum, stands on a natural causeway across the marshy valley of the River Ouse. The

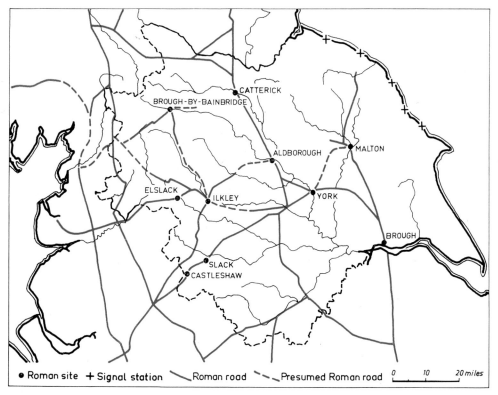

Fig. 39 *Map of Roman roads, forts and signal stations*

63

causeway is formed by a glacial moraine through which the river later cut a narrow gorge. Thus the site commands the main natural bridge across the Vale of York, linking the eastern and western halves of the county. At the same time the Ouse was navigable up to this point and sea-going ships could sail right up to the walls of the camp, bringing essential supplies for the troops stationed there. In this way large shipments of grain were brought from the rich agricultural areas of the East Anglian fenlands. Iron could be brought from the ore deposits of Lincolnshire to the south; lead from Derbyshire, and essential building materials like stone and slate from the hills of the West Riding. There is also ample evidence that olive oil and wine were imported from the Continent.

Roman troops were already permanently stationed at York by the reign of the Emperor Vespasian as part of the drive against the Brigantes in A.D. 71–74. The fortress was designed to accommodate a legion, enclosing an area of some 50 acres and laid out as a rectangle with rounded corners (fig. 40). The Roman army was divided into legionary and auxiliary troops. A legion was a body of troops about 6,000 strong composed of full citizens of the Empire. An auxiliary unit numbered 500 or 1,000 men and was recruited from men of more backward areas. In the main it was the auxiliaries who took the brunt of the fighting, while the legionaries were held in reserve. The auxiliaries were likely to be drawn from far and wide within the Empire, for it was Roman policy to send them far away from their homelands so that there should be no conflicting loyalties.

Just how wide this recruitment area could be is demonstrated by a military diploma of the time of the Emperor Hadrian (A.D. 117–38) found at Stannington, 4 miles west of Sheffield. The diploma, now fragmentary,

consisted of two bronze plates joined together, and records the granting of citizenship to veteran soldiers, their wives, and their children. Amongst the auxiliaries named as being in Britain were the *Nervii* and the *Tungrians* from Belgium, the *Batavians* from Holland, the *Vangiones* from west Germany, the *Aquitanians* from south-west France, the *Asturians* and *Vardulli* from northern Spain, the *Dalmatians* from Yugoslavia, and the *Ulpians* from Rumania.

The legion stationed at York was the Ninth. This had seen distinguished service in Spain and had been given the title *Hispana* to commemorate these deeds. Between A.D. 79 and 85 the fortifications at York were made more permanent. The first rampart round the fort had been a hasty affair of clay and sand laid down on green timbers. Agricola now replaced this with a more permanent rampart of stiff clay, faced with turf on a squared timber frame. Timber towers were built at intervals along its length. The internal buildings were timber-framed with walls of wattle and daub. To reduce the risk of fire large cooking-ovens were built near the rampart, some distance away from the wooden buildings.

LEAD-MINING

The system of roads which Agricola had constructed led to exploitation of the raw materials of the West Riding. Lead has already been mentioned as being imported from Derbyshire, but soon the lead deposits of Wharfedale, Nidderdale, and Swaledale were being worked. Two ingots of lead, usually known as 'pigs', were found on Hayshaw Moor between Pateley Bridge and Ilkley. These weighed 155 and 156 lb respectively and were inscribed: IMP. CAES. DOMITIANO AUG. COS. VII—'The seventh consulship of the Emperor Domitian, Caesar, Augustus'. This was the Roman method of dating the

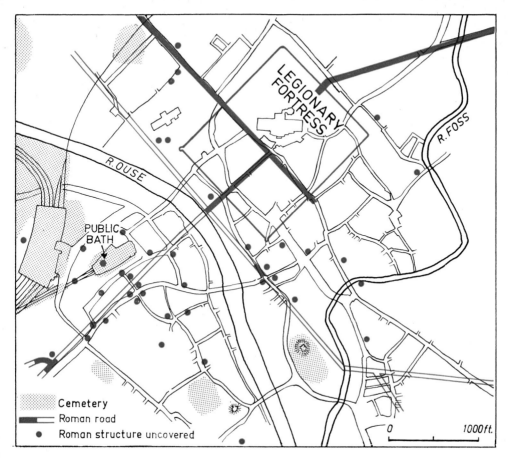

Fig. 40 *Plan of Eburacum [York] (after R.C.H.M.)*

ingots, for the seventh consulship of Domitian's reign fell in the year A.D. 81.

Lead was also mined at Greenhowe Hill, between Pateley Bridge and Grassington, and another 'pig', bearing the name of the Emperor Trajan, was found in this region. By the reign of Hadrian (A.D. 117–38) the lead deposits in Swaledale were being mined and another 'pig' inscribed with the emperor's name [H]ADRIAN was found at Hurst Mines. The 'pigs' carry the emperor's name, for the State owned all the mining rights in Yorkshire.

YORKSHIRE UNDER TRAJAN

In A.D. 85–86 the Agricolan governorship ended. Troops were withdrawn from Britain to fight on the Danube and the Roman position was inevitably weakened. The Brigantes, seizing the opportunity to strike against the Romans when their garrisons were depleted, revolted. Even so, their success was short-

65

Fig. 41 *The commemorative tablet from King's Square, York*

lived for, under Trajan (A.D. 98–117), many of the earlier forts like Malton, which had been founded by Agricola in about A.D. 79, were reconstructed. At Malton the earlier ditch was now filled and a new defensive system created with a stone rampart behind two deep ditches. About the same time the defences at York were similarly rebuilt. A fragment of a fine commemorative tablet (fig. 41) found in King's Square records this task and gives a date of A.D. 107–8 for the work. To this Trajanic period belong half a double door and one of the two guard-chamber basements at the south-west gate on the side overlooking the river. Interval towers and an angle tower were built in stone, and a 5-foot curtain wall was constructed with Magnesian limestone probably brought from the Tadcaster region.

To the reign of the Emperor Trajan also belong the four camps which can be seen on the edge of the Tabular hills at Cawthorn, 4 miles north of Pickering. As can be seen from the plan, fig. 42, Camp D cuts into and is therefore later than Camp C, and Camp B cuts into Camp A and is therefore later than that construction. They were, in fact, 'practice camps'. During the exercises the troops living in Camp C constructed Camp A and, at a later date, troops living in Camp B constructed Camp D. The soldiers taking part in these exercises were legionary troops, presumably from the Ninth Legion at York, for they possessed the *ballista*. This was a device like a giant catapult for hurling stones and was a weapon not given to the auxiliaries during this period.

THE ARRIVAL OF THE SIXTH LEGION

The fate of the Ninth Legion still remains something of a mystery. Perhaps it suffered a disastrous defeat at the hands of the northern tribes, or disgraced itself in battle and was disbanded. Nothing is certain. We do know, however, that the Ninth Legion was replaced at York by the Sixth Legion, which was brought over from Germany by Platorius

66

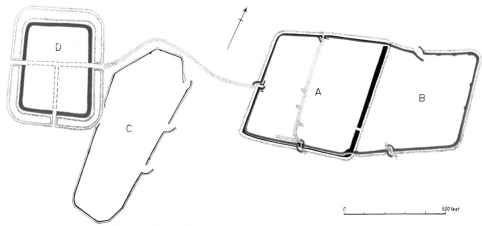

Fig. 42 *Plan of the Roman practice camps at Cawthorn*

Nepos, whose governorship began in A.D. 122.

The Sixth Legion was now to be stationed at York until the fourth century. Monuments recording the stay are numerous. From the Mount at York comes a tombstone depicting Caeresius Augustinus, a soldier of the Sixth Legion, his wife and their two sons, with the inscription beneath:

D(IS) . M(ANIBUS) . FLAVIAE AUGUSTINAE .
VIXIT . AN(NOS) . XXXVIIII . M(ENSES) . VII . D(IES) . XI . FILIUS
S . . . NIUS AUGUSTINUS. VIXIT AN(NUM) . I D(IES) III
. . . VIXIT . AN(NUM) I. M(ENSES) VIIII D(IES) V CAERESIUS
. . . INUS VET(ERANUS) LEG(IONIS) VI VIC(TRICIS) CONIUGI CARI
SSIMAE ET . SIBI . F(ACIUNDUM) . C(URAVIT).

'To the spirits of the departed. To Flavia Augustina. She lived 39 years, 7 months, 11 days. Her son . . . nius Augustinus, lived 1 year, 3 days . . . lived 1 year, 9 months, five days. Caeresius (August)inus, veteran of the Sixth Legion Victorious, had (this stone) made for his dearest wife and himself.'

A dedication tablet found in Toft Green is particularly well preserved. This was inscribed:

'To the holy god Serapis, Claudius Hieronymianus, legate of the Sixth Legion Victorious, built this temple from the gound.'

DEO . SANCTO
SERAPI
TEMPLUM . A SO
LO FECIT
CL(AUDIUS) . HIERONY
MIANUS . LEG(ATUS)
LEG(IONIS) . VI . VIC(TRICIS)

FURTHER REVOLTS

History was to repeat itself more than once. In A.D. 196 the Governor of Britain, Clodius Albinus, transferred a large body of troops to the Continent in an effort to gain the throne from Septimius Severus. The attempt was unsuccessful, but once more it gave the Caledonian tribes of central and northern Scotland a chance to strike while the Roman garrisons were below strength. The combined forces of the *Caledonii* and the *Maeatae* swept down through northern England, spreading destruction certainly as far south as York. The year 197 therefore saw rebuilding operations in many of the northern forts. The forts at Ilkley and Bowes were repaired and at York a new stone wall was constructed with towers rebuilt to include artillery emplacements. The defences thus repaired, Severus with his two sons, Geta and Caracalla, set out to punish the northern tribes. The campaign was successful, but the conditions which were then imposed seem to have been too severe and a second revolt broke out in A.D. 210–11. In the latter year Severus himself died at York.

PETUARIA

Though Yorkshire had now been under Roman occupation for a hundred and fifty years, the influence of the Roman way of life upon the native population was probably not great. In the outlying native villages and farmsteads the closest contact with the Romans was the regular visit of the tax collector. For under Roman rule the price of peace was the cost of keeping the army fed. The only town to show any real adoption of Roman ways at an early date was Petuaria, the modern Brough-on-Humber.

The town was well placed on the direct roads to the legionary fortress at York and the important fort at Malton. Lying also on the River Humber, it commanded wide communications both by land and sea. At the beginning of the second century the huts of the original native settlement were replaced by foundations of Roman-style buildings, though many of these were never completed. By A.D. 150–80 the settlement was given a defensive system with a turf rampart and triple ditches. Some of the internal buildings were completed in stone but by now the exact position of many of the foundations was no longer known. As a result several buildings were found to have been built at an angle to the original foundations. Some time after A.D. 180 the defensive rampart was rebuilt in stone.

There is also evidence that the civil administration at Petuaria was one not normally found in the ordinary town. In the reign of Antoninus Pius, Petuaria boasted an *aedilis*, an unusually high-ranking official for a town of this size. To commemorate his election, the aedilis, one M. Ulpius Ianuarius, built a theatre stage for the community, at his own expense. This was a remarkable gesture, for comparable theatres have been found in only three other British towns, Verulamium (St Albans), Canterbury, and Colchester. Here was a deliberate attempt to bring to this regional capital of the *Parisi* something of the life of the Romanized south.

Even so the Romanization of Petuaria was far from complete. To the north of the town, by the side of the road to York, the grave of a native priest was uncovered. With the skeleton lay the remains of a small wooden bucket bound with iron hoops. The handle had been decorated with a bronze escutcheon in the shape of a human head, probably modelled on a local native of the second century. Two bronze and iron sceptres had also been placed in the grave, both of which ended in bronze mounts depicting helmeted heads. These are of native workmanship, but an attempt has been made to reproduce the appearance of the local Roman trooper. Both sceptres had been deliberately twisted before being placed in the grave. This action was no doubt intended to symbolize the destruction of the priest's powers at death. This was essentially a non-Roman belief and, like the custom of placing a bucket with the dead, shows that native beliefs still survived despite outward signs of Romanization.

THE CANABAE AND COLONIA AT YORK

Roman influence also spread from the civilian settlements that grew up outside the Roman forts. A mixture of traders and camp followers were naturally attracted by the wealth and power of the Roman garrisons. In the course of time more permanent settlements grew up in the shadow of the forts.

One such settlement or *canabae* grew up outside the north-western and south-eastern sides of the fortress at York. The traders here set up their booths on land leased from the Legion. Unfortunately the modern city covers much of this settlement and its actual extent is hard to define.

A second and more important settlement grew up across the River Ouse along the south-west road leading from York to Tadcaster. Amongst the earliest monuments which belong to it are a dedicatory slab to Silvanus set up by Lucius Celerinius Vitalis, a clerk of the Ninth Legion, and a tombstone of another soldier of the Ninth, Lucius Duccus Rufinus, who held the rank of standard-bearer. The settlement quickly grew in prosperity and by A.D. 237 had received a charter which established it as an independent chartered town or *colonia*. The evidence for this comes not from York itself, but from an altar in Bordeaux, which was set up by Marcus Aurelius Lunaris, a merchant of York, who was probably engaged in the wine trade with southern France. The Colonia became the capital of *Britannia Inferior*, encompassing the territories of the *Brigantes*, the *Parisi*, and the *Coritani* to the south.

ISURIUM BRIGANTUM
AND CATARACTONIUM

To the north-west, Isurium Brigantum, the modern Aldborough, became the flourishing regional capital of the Brigantes. The town covered an area of some 55 acres and was surrounded by a sandstone wall with artillery towers set along its length. The houses were of timber, built on stone foundations, and mosaic floors have been found in several of them. These floors depict scenes and designs built up with small coloured cubes of stone and pottery called *tesserae*. One of the mosaics depicts a wolf and twins under a fig tree. It was originally raised up on the pillars of a hypocaust—the Roman form of central heating, whereby hot air passed beneath the floor through a system of flues to heat the room above. To the south of the west gate lay the public baths. The large deposit of oyster, cockle, and mussel shells in this area records the well-known Roman taste for shell-fish.

To the north of Aldborough, at Catterick Bridge, lay the town of Cataractonium, sited on the River Swale. In the area so far examined second-century timber-built shops and workshops have been found on the main east-west road. A more complex building with stone foundations, which in its final form covered about an acre, included a bath-house and fountain. Though the peace of Yorkshire had been broken more than once, a wall was apparently not built round the town until the middle of the third century. The whole town plan was altered in the early part of the fourth century and there are clear signs that the township was still flourishing at the end of the century.

TROUBLED TIMES

The inhabitants of Cataractonium may have lived relatively peaceful lives, but other parts of Yorkshire were not so fortunate. By the middle of the third century, when a defensive wall was finally considered necessary, sea-raiders were becoming sufficiently persistent for the Emperor Diocletian to set up a special branch of the navy to deal with this new threat. Its first commander was Carausius. Unfortunately, the temptation to use the force for his own ends proved too strong. In 287 Carausius proclaimed himself Emperor of Britain. His self-appointed reign was short-lived, for in 293 he was murdered by Allectus, who then himself usurped the throne.

Again the Roman troops, whose presence alone kept the peace in northern Britain, were withdrawn. Allectus gathered his troops in southern England, but was defeated by Constantius in 296. Once more the northern tribes seized their opportunity and swept south. The troubled times are well documented by hoards of coins hidden away, but never recovered. At Methill, near Warter in the East Riding, one hoard contained as many as 6,000 coins dating from A.D. 253–75. In the West Riding, caves like Victoria cave near Settle and Dowkerbottom cave between Arncliffe and Kilnsey in Wharfedale tell the same story. The coins recovered from the caves span the period A.D. 253–340. Besides pottery many fine bronze brooches were recovered, as well as jet and glass beads and armlets, bone pins and perforated spoons. These add up to something more than the everyday equipment of the local shepherd. Either the caves were robbers' dens or places of refuge when hostile tribesmen were pillaging the district. Whichever way the evidence is interpreted, the caves speak of troubled times deep in the heart of the Pennine Hills.

The defences at York were now rebuilt on a far grander scale. Six interval towers and two vast angle towers were built to dominate the river front. Constantius did not long survive these rebuilding operations. In 306 he died at York and his son Constantine was proclaimed emperor. For a short while Yorkshire was to enjoy a fitful peace.

THE VILLAS AT LANGTON AND RUDSTON

By the fourth century the country estates of eastern Yorkshire were thriving. At least twelve villas are known from the territory of the *Parisi*. Their prosperity was largely based on corn production and no doubt the surplus corn which did not find its way to York or the fort at Malton was sent to the markets of Petuaria.

The villa at Langton has a long history. The first occupation on the site was a simple native homestead dating to the first-century. By the fourth century, however, we have a complete farm. The farmhouse contained two heated rooms and a small bath-house. The main product was corn and all the subsidiary buildings needed to deal with the crop are present. The corn was dried in a simple furnace, threshed on a specially prepared platform, and ground into flour in a circular mill. There was also a storehouse for the seed grain and the flour. Coins recovered on the site show that the villa was flourishing in the earlier part of the fourth century. No less than thirty-three of the 104 decipherable coins belong to the years A.D. 320–64. In a short while the farmer was able to add two new rooms to his house and a veranda facing south-west.

The farm was not to enjoy a completely peaceful life. There are signs that a fire had at one stage destroyed several buildings. But the farm recovered, for after 370, coins of Valentinian I and the later emperors are numerous, and the farm was probably still supplying wheat to the Malton fort at least until the beginning of the fifth century.

The villa at Rudston has received considerable attention recently and parts of three mosaic pavements have now been removed to Hull Museum. In the fourth century the Villa boasted a fine bath-house in its east wing. First one entered the unheated dressing-room with its mosaic pavement figuring an aquatic scene with dolphins, fish, and an open oyster. Round the edge was a border of waterlilies and at each end a panel of trees. From the dressing-room the bather passed first into the warm room and then into the hot room. This lay over a hypocaust system the stoking chamber of which lay to the north-west. From the hot room he leapt straight into the cold plunge and so back into the dressing-room.

Mosaic floors were set into two of the main rooms of the farmhouse. One covered an area 15 feet by 10½ feet and is set out on an ambitious scale (fig. 43). In the central circle we have Venus carrying the apple which Paris had presented to her. With her to the left is an attendant Triton and to the right is her mirror. The bordering panels depict wild animals. In one is a leopard with a shield above. In the next is a wild bull with the inscription TAURUS (H)OMICIDA or 'the bull

that kills men'. In the third is a lion transfixed by a spear. In the fourth a stag in a pine forest. At the corners are birds pecking fruit. The remaining space is taken up with human figures of which three survive. One is a nymph, the other two go with the wild animals and are huntsmen: one leaning on a spear, the other casting a net. At each end of the pavement there is a single rectangular panel depicting a pair of plants each growing out of a two-handled vase which flank a bust of Mercury. Only one of these panels now survives.

The second pavement uses a completely geometric design to cover a space of some 12 feet square. This formal design has been well executed by the native craftsman and was obviously far more suited to his talents than the more ambitious figure work of the Venus pavement.

THE GATHERING STORM: FRANKS, SAXONS AND SCOTS

By the middle of the fourth century raids by marauding parties from Ireland and western Scotland were becoming a real problem in the north-west of England. In A.D. 367–9 a concerted attack was launched by the *Franks* and *Saxons* from the east and the *Atecotti* and *Scoti* from the west. The Roman fort at Malton was damaged and no doubt the fire at the Langton farm dates to this attack.

These raids underlined a weakness in the Roman defensive system. The main threat now came from the sea and it was obvious that a new system was needed for giving adequate warning of any impending raid. The modern early-warning radar station on the moors at Fylingdales has early forerunners, for signal stations were now set up by Count Theodosius along the coast at Huntcliff near Saltburn, Kettleness, Ravenscar, Scarborough, and Filey (*see* fig. 39). These were built not

Fig. 43 *The Venus mosaic from Rudston*

to defend the coast but to give the alarm to inland garrisons like that at Malton, where a mobile cavalry force was stationed.

The signal stations were built to a standard pattern and the best-preserved example is that in Goldsborough Pasture, about half a mile from the sea at Kettleness (fig. 44). The outer

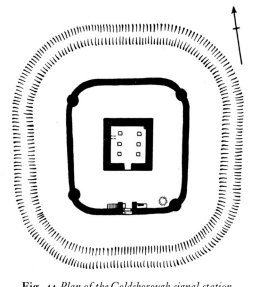

Fig. 44 *Plan of the Goldsborough signal station*

wall was 4 feet thick at the base and enclosed a rectangular area of 105 feet with rounded corners strengthened by circular turrets. The gateway was set in the south wall and led into an unpaved courtyard, about 30 feet across, which surrounded the central signal tower. This was a square wooden tower set on stone foundations. It was built in two or three stories and was 90 to 100 feet high. The whole structure was encircled by a ditch separated from the outer wall by a berm. A sure supply of water was provided by a well sunk 8½ feet into the courtyard.

The men who manned the tower seem to have enjoyed a varied diet of meat, fish, and fowl. The floor was littered with assorted bones of pigs, oxen, goats, deer, hare, rabbits, and small birds, as well as fish bones, crab shells, mussels, limpets, whelks, and periwinkles.

Sometime early in the fifth century the tower, like the others along the coast, was overwhelmed and burnt to the ground. The evidence of the final stand is vivid. In the ruins of the tower the excavators found the skeleton of a short thick-set man who had fallen across the smouldering fire of an open hearth, probably stabbed in the back. He lay face down, his left hand behind his back with a bronze ring still encircling his finger, his right hand touching the wall. The skeleton of a taller man lay face down near the feet of the first and beneath him lay the skeleton of a large and powerful dog, its head against the man's throat and its paws across his shoulders. The dog, too, had defended to the last.

THE END OF THE ROMAN MILITARY OCCUPATION

With the destruction of the signal stations the end of the Roman military occupation is in sight. In 407 Constantius III withdrew the Roman garrisons to the Continent for the last time. Three years later the Emperor Honorius could only tell the British urban communities to provide for their own defence

Fig. 45 *The Catterick Bridge buckle*

72

as best they could. Yet, despite the destruction of the signal stations and the sea-raids, it would be wrong to think that the Romano-British townships and country estates were immediately destroyed. Many seem to have prospered for a while before finally falling into decay.

Some of the richer communities in eastern Yorkshire employed Anglian mercenaries to defend them. German mercenaries were already known in the Roman army. A buckle of a distinctive type made only in the Rhineland for German troops in the Roman army was found at Catterick Bridge in the Roman levels (fig. 45). When the army withdrew some mercenaries may have been induced to settle in Yorkshire with gifts of land. Close to the fortress at York there are two early Anglian cemeteries belonging to such settlements, and at Elmswell near Driffield early Anglian and late or sub-Roman remains were found together. For over three centuries the Romans had forced the inhabitants of Yorkshire to pay for peace. The tax collector may now have gone, but peace had still to be bought.

SOME BOOKS TO READ

The following list is not exhaustive. It merely includes some general books which may help to place the Yorkshire finds in better perspective, and a few of the major works on prehistoric and Roman Yorkshire. The many regional surveys and site reports which have been written in book and shorter article cannot be included here, but several are quoted in connexion with individual sites in the short gazetteer which follows. In particular the volumes of the *Yorkshire Archaeological Society* and the *Transactions of the Scarborough and District Archaeological Society* are invaluable sources of detailed information.

J. G. D. Clark, *World Prehistory—An Outline* (Cambridge University Press, 1962)

J. G. D. Clark, *Prehistoric England* (Batsford, 1963)

M. K. Clark, *A Gazetteer of Roman Remains in East Yorkshire* (Roman Malton and District Report, no. 5, 1935)

F. Elgee, *Early Man in North East Yorkshire* (John Bellows, 1930)

F. and H. W. Elgee, *The Archaeology of Yorkshire* (Methuen, 1933)

W. Greenwell, *British Barrows* (Oxford University Press, 1877)

J. Hawkes, *A Guide to the Prehistoric and Roman Monuments of England and Wales* (Chatto & Windus, 1951)

J. and C. F. C. Hawkes, *Prehistoric Britain* (Penguin Books, 1958)

J. R. Mortimer, *Forty Years' Researches in British and Saxon Burial Mounds of East Yorkshire* (A. Brown & Sons, 1905)

I. A. Richmond, *Roman Britain* (Penguin Books, 1963)

A. L. F. Rivet, *Town and Country in Roman Britain* (Hutchinson, 1958)

N. Thomas, *A Guide to Prehistoric England* (Batsford, 1960)

Maps, of course, are essential. The Ordnance Survey one-inch and quarter-inch maps are most useful when searching for and visiting sites in the countryside. The Ordnance Survey also produce two period maps: *A Map of Ancient Britain* and *A Map of Roman Britain* both highly relevant to the archaeology of Yorkshire.

Sites to Visit

The following short list does not attempt to include every prehistoric and Roman site in Yorkshire. These are far too numerous to be covered in a book of this size. It is hoped, however, that the list may be of use as an introduction to a few of the better-known field monuments and so help in the identification of others which for want of space cannot now be included.

It should be remembered that many archaeological sites lie on private land and in these cases permission to visit the site should first be obtained.

The sites have been arranged alphabetically under Ridings.

YORK

ROMAN FORTRESS, CANABAE AND COLONIA

DATE: Late first century—fifth century A.D.

PUBLICATION: Royal Commission on Historical Monuments, Vol I *Eburacum* Roman York (1962).

The Roman fortress and outlying settlements now lie almost entirely concealed beneath the modern city.

The Fortress

The Legionary Fortress, covering an area of about 50 acres, was founded in A.D. 71–72 by Cerialis commanding the Ninth Legion. It was arranged in the form of a rectangle with rounded corners. Stonegate and Petergate still preserve the line of two of its main streets, the *via praetoria* and the *via principalis* respectively. The first ramparts were rebuilt by Agricola in stiff clay, faced with turf, and timber towers were added. In 107–8 the defences were again rebuilt, but this time in stone.

By A.D. 122 the Ninth Legion had been replaced by the Sixth. Following the northern revolt, further rebuilding was necessary in 197. The new wall was 6 feet thick and the towers were rebuilt and equipped for artillery.

In the fourth century the defences were completely remodelled and the fortress took on a most imposing appearance. Six interval towers and two massive angle towers were built to dominate the river. Most of the visible remains of the fortress belong to this phase.

The west angle tower can be seen in the museum gardens. It still survives to a height of 19 feet, capped by later medieval additions. A stretch of the fortress wall, 35 feet in length, can also be seen surviving to a height of 13 feet.

The east angle tower can be seen behind the Merchant Taylors' Hall. This is all that remains of an internal tower surviving now to a height of 7½ feet. The south angle tower, which lies mainly under Feasegate, is partially preserved in the basement of Hart's Store.

There is also a bath-house under the Mail Coach Inn in St Sampson's Square and partly preserved in the cellars of the inn. This structure also dates to the fourth century.

The Canabae

A civil settlement or *Canabae* lay outside the fortress mainly on its north-western and south-eastern sides with a more scattered occupation to the north-east. This lay on land leased from the garrison, but it is almost entirely covered by the modern city.

The Colonia

Across the River Ouse another settlement grew up along the south-west road to Tadcaster. By A.D. 237 this had become a chartered town or *Colonia* and was the capital of Britannia Inferior, including the provinces of the Brigantes to the north, the Parisi to the east and the Coritani to the south. No structures now survive above ground.

A great wealth of sculpture, tombstones, inscribed slabs and small finds from Roman York can be seen in the Yorkshire Museum.

See fig. 40 and Chapter Seven.

EAST RIDING

BROUGH-ON-HUMBER

ROMAN FORT AND TOWN
DATE: First–fourth century A.D.
MAP REF.: SE/937267
PUBLICATION: J. S. Wacher, 'Petuaria. New evidence for the Roman Town and its earlier fort', *Antiquaries Journal*, XL, 58–64.
DIRECTIONS: 10¼ m. W. of Kingston upon Hull. Take the A63 from Hull, turning left just beyond Welton into the village of Brough.

The Roman town of Petuaria and tribal capital of the Parisi. Little can be seen on the ground. The earliest occupation consisted of a military fort with a settlement to the south. Early in the second century the fort went out of use and Petuaria became a civil provincial town. An attempt was made to include both the native settlement and the fort into one town plan. The native huts were cleared and foundations put down for Roman-style buildings, though many of these were completed only at a later date. The new town was defended by a turf rampart and triple ditch.

The town seems to have been at its most prosperous during the second century. A theatre stage was given to the community by the Aedile, M. Ulpius Januarius, and towards the end of the century the rampart was rebuilt in stone.

Despite later building alterations, by the end of the fourth century Petuaria had ceased to be of much importance.

See Chapter Seven.

CALLIS WOLD

ROUND BARROWS
DATE: 1800–1000 B.C.
MAP REF.: Around SE/830555
PUBLICATION: J. R. Mortimer, *Forty Years' Researches in British and Saxon Burial Mounds of East Yorkshire* (1905), 153–71.
DIRECTIONS: 4½ m. N.E. of Pocklington, stretching S.E. from a point approximately 7 miles E. of Stamford Bridge along the A166 in the direction of Millington Heights.

Originally there were eighteen round barrows on the wold, but those which survive have all been damaged by the plough.

One mound covered two collared urns, set side by side. Both stood upright, containing cremations, and a small string of jet and faience beads had been placed in one of the urns.

Another barrow covered a crouched inhumation with a food vessel and stone battle-axe. This mound had been built over the remains of two concentric rings of wooden stakes, 21½ and 28 feet in diameter.

Other barrows in the group contained broken beakers, burials with food vessels, collared urns, incense cups and a fine jet necklace.

DANE'S DYKE

DEFENSIVE EARTHWORK
DATE: *c.* 300 B.C.–A.D. 100
MAP REF.: TA/216694
DIRECTIONS: The main road from Bridlington to Flamborough (B1255) cuts through the dike about ½ m. from its southern end, ¾ m. W. of Flamborough.

The dike was probably built in the Iron Age; 2½ miles long, it runs north and south from coast to coast, cutting off an area of Flamborough Head about 5 miles square. The bank is 18 feet high in places. The wide ditch is on the western side and a counterscarp bank is clearly visible.

See Chapter Six.

DANES' GRAVES

BARROW CEMETERY
DATE: *c.* third century B.C.
MAP REF.: TA/018633
PUBLICATION: W. Greenwell, 'Early Iron Age Burials in Yorkshire', *Archaeologia*, LX, 251–324.
DIRECTIONS: 3½ m. N. of Driffield. Take the Driffield–Langtoft road (B1249). The barrows lie about ½ m. E. of the road in a plantation S. of the track leading to Westfield Farm.

There were probably once 500 barrows in the cemetery, but only a small number can now be seen. The barrows are small, averaging between 8 and 30 feet across and no more than 3 feet high. Some are surrounded by a ditch. The dead were buried in a contracted position in a simple pit dug into the underlying chalk. Many graves contained nothing except the body, but in some a pot was found, sometimes containing a leg of pork. Other finds included several iron brooches, two bronze brooches, bracelets of bronze, iron and jet and a glass bead.

One large grave contained the skeletons of two men and the dismantled remains of a two-wheeled chariot.

See Chapter Six.

DUGGLEBY HOWE

ROUND BARROW

DATE: 2100–1700 B.C.

MAP REF.: SE/881669

PUBLICATION: J. R. Mortimer, *Forty Years' Researches in British and Saxon Burial Mounds of East Yorkshire* (1905), 23–42.

DIRECTIONS: 2¼ m. E.S.E. of North Grimston, S.E. of Duggleby, just E. of the Duggleby–Sledmere road (B1253).

The barrow dates to the late neolithic period and is one of the largest round barrows in Britain. It still stands 20 feet high, though the height must once have been nearer 30 feet.

The mound covered a deep grave pit and a shallower grave, each containing inhumation burials. These were accompanied by stone and antler tools, and a simple bowl-shaped pot. More skeletons were found in the mound as well as a large number of cremation burials. Under the influence of Beaker immigrants from the Continent the earlier forms of burial customs were often modified. The mixture of different types of burial in this mound dates to this period of changing beliefs.

See Chapter Three.

RUDSTON

STANDING STONE

DATE: 2000–1500 B.C.

MAP REF.: TA/097677

PUBLICATION: *Archaeological Journal*, CV, 72 and pl. IX.

DIRECTIONS: The stone stands in Rudston churchyard on the road from Sledmere to Bridlington (B1253), 5 m. W. of Bridlington.

This is the tallest single standing stone in Britain, 25½ feet high, 6 feet wide and 2¼ feet thick. The nearest source for this gritstone would be outcrops some 10 miles to the north at Cayton Bay.

See Chapter Three.

SHARP HOWES

ROUND BARROWS

DATE: 1700–1300 B.C.

MAP REF.: TA/049777

PUBLICATION: W. Greenwell, 'Recent Researches in Barrows in Yorkshire, Wiltshire, Berkshire, etc.', *Archaeologia*, LII, 5–10.

DIRECTIONS: 4½ m. S.W. of Filey, 1¼ m. S. of Folkton. Take the A1039 to Flixton, turn S.

along the road from Flixton to Burton Fleming. The barrows lie just E. of this road.

There are five barrows here forming a well-defined cemetery. The largest of the barrows lies at the southern end of the group, 80 feet across and 8 feet high. This has been built with chalk slabs covered with a layer of earth and capped with chalk rubble. A grave at the centre of the barrow contained a contracted skeleton with a food vessel.

Burials with food vessels were also found beneath the other mounds and in the most northerly an unburnt flint knife and bone pin had been placed with a cremation in a small grave found within the body of the mound.

STAPLE HOWE

FARMSTEAD

DATE: Begins 500 B.C.

MAP REF.: SE/898749

PUBLICATION: T. C. M. Brewster, *The Excavation of Staple Howe* (1963).

DIRECTIONS: 7 m. N.E. of Malton, just over 1 m. S.E. of Knapton, S. of the main Malton–Filey road (A64) in Knapton Plantation, about 1½ m. E. of the junction of the B1258 with the A64. A path has been made to the site.

The farmstead was set within a palisade running round the top of the natural hill of chalk known as Staple Howe. At first this enclosed a single oval hut, 30 feet long and 20 feet across. Its walls were of stone or chalk and its roof was gabled. Remains of a clay oven and hearth were found inside.

At a later stage this first hut was replaced by two round huts and a granary (*see* fig. 28). A circle of post-holes with a central post showed that these huts had walls of timber and their roofs were conical. Each had a porch facing south-east. Hearths and ovens were found, and in one the remains of an upright loom. The granary was set in the centre of the farm on one of the highest points. It consisted of a small hut set on a platform supported by five stout posts.

Besides the remains of domestic and wild animals a considerable quantity of burnt grain was recovered, and a sample of this was dated by means of the Carbon 14 dating method to 440 ± 150 B.C. Large quantities of pottery were found as well as objects of jet, bone and antler. Only two pieces of iron were found: an iron ring and part of an iron pin. Bronze objects were more numerous and included a type of razor which on the Continent dates to before 500 B.C.

The positions of two of the huts and the granary site have been marked with concrete posts.

See Chapter Six.

TOWTHORPE

ROUND BARROWS

DATE: 1800–1300 B.C.

MAP REF.: Especially between SE/878638 and SE/900646

PUBLICATION: J. R. Mortimer, *Forty Years' Researches in British and Saxon Burial Mounds of East Yorkshire* (1905), 1–43.

DIRECTIONS: 7½ m. S.E. of Malton, 2 m. S. of Duggleby along the green road from Aldro to Sledmere, especially between the B1248 and B1253 in Towthorpe Plantation.

This line of barrows suggests that a prehistoric trackway may once have passed along the line of the present green road.

Most of the barrows have been opened. In one a fine bronze dagger of the type found in early 'Wessex Culture' graves was found with a perforated stone hammer and flint knife, in a grave dug for an extended inhumation. A similar dagger was found with a crouched skeleton in one of the other barrows in the group.

A large number of burials, inhumations and cremations, have been recorded from the barrows, including graves containing beaker and food vessel pottery.

WHARRAM PERCY

ROUND BARROWS

DATE: 1700–1000 B.C.

MAP REF.: SE/837637

PUBLICATION: J. R. Mortimer, *Forty Years' Researches in British and Saxon Burial Mounds of East Yorkshire* (1905), 44–52.

DIRECTIONS: 7 m. S.E. of Malton, 2½ m. S. of North Grimston and ½ m. W. of Wharram Percy House.

Six barrows stand in line, suggesting that a prehistoric trackway may once have passed this way. All have been opened. In one a cremation had been placed in a grave together with a food vessel, a ring-headed bone pin, a flint knife and a flint punch.

Burials with food vessels and collared urns were also found in the other barrows of the cemetery.

WILLERBY WOLD

LONG BARROW

DATE: 2500–1700 B.C.

MAP REF.: TA/029761

PUBLICATION: T. G. Manby, 'The Excavation of the Willerby Wold Long Barrow, East Riding of Yorkshire', *Proceedings of the Prehistoric Society*, XXIX, 173–205.

DIRECTIONS: 7 m. S. of Scarborough, 2 m. S.S.E. of Staxton. Take the Staxton-Langtoft road (B1249), then turn left along the road leading to Fordon. The barrow is about 1 m. from the turning and just S. of the road.

The barrow is 133 feet long and 4 feet high at its eastern end. Excavations have shown that the mound was originally of trapezoidal shape, 122 feet long and 35 feet wide at its eastern end, with side ditches.

The mound had been built over the site of a trapezoidal mortuary enclosure. This had been marked out with a continuous narrow ditch except at the eastern end, where a concave row of upright posts was set into a narrow bedding trench. These posts had been deliberately burnt down before the mound was built.

The mortuary enclosure had been used to store the bodies of the dead until the time came to build the mound. The bodies, now decomposed and disarticulated, were placed between the walls of a crematorium constructed at the eastern end of the enclosure, and heaped over with chalk rubble mixed with timber. The mound was then built with chalk taken from the side ditches. Finally the crematorium deposit, which now resembled a horizontal lime kiln, was fired, cremating the bodies and turning some of the rubble into lime.

See Chapter Two.

WILLY HOWE

ROUND BARROW

DATE: 2100–1700 B.C.

MAP REF.: TA/063724

PUBLICATION: W. Greenwell, 'Recent Researches in Barrows in Yorkshire, Wiltshire, Berkshire, etc.', *Archaeologia*, LII, 22–27.

DIRECTIONS: 3½ m. N.W. of Rudston, 1½ m. W. of Burton Fleming.

This round barrow is 120 feet across and 24 feet high. It was excavated in 1857 by Lord Londesborough and again in 1887 by Greenwell. A grave pit 4 feet long, 2 feet 8 inches wide and over 12 feet deep was found, but no burials or datable objects were found. Its resemblance in size and shape to *Duggleby Howe* suggests that it may belong to the late neolithic period.

NORTH RIDING

ALLAN TOPS

FIELDS AND CAIRNS
DATE: Uncertain
MAP REF.: NZ/828028
DIRECTIONS: 6¼ m. S.W. of Whitby, 1½ m. S. of Grosmont, ½ m. N.E. of Beck Hole.

A number of enclosures and field walls can be seen here. Amongst them cluster over seventy small cairns. The purpose of these cairns is still unknown and they are not necessarily of the same date as the enclosures.

BLAKEY TOPPING

STONE CIRCLE
DATE: 1600–1000 B.C.
MAP REF.: SE/873934
DIRECTIONS: 7¼ m. N.E. of Pickering, 2¾ m. N.E. of Lockton, about 1¼ m. E. of the Pickering-Whitby road (A169).

On the south-western side of Blakey Topping are the remains of a stone circle. Only three of the stones now survive. These are about 6 feet high. In several places depressions can be seen marking the sockets where other stones in the circle once stood.

BOLTBY SCAR

PROMONTORY FORT
DATE: 300 B.C.–A.D. 100
MAP REF.: SE/506857
DIRECTIONS: 7 m. W. of Helmsley, 1¾ m. N.W. of Cold Kirby.

The site is naturally defended on the western side by a steep cliff face. A semicircular bank and ditch had been dug on the eastern side to enclose an area of about 2½ acres, though little now survives due to recent bulldozing.

A pair of Early Bronze Age gold ear-rings were found in the old ground surface beneath the bank and three Bronze Age round barrows could once be seen within the area enclosed by the fort. One of these covered a cremation in a collared urn.

CANA

HENGE MONUMENT
DATE: 2000–1500 B.C.
MAP REF.: SE/361718
PUBLICATION: N. Thomas, 'The Thornborough Circles near Ripon, North Riding, *Yorkshire Archaeological Journal*, XXXVIII, 425–45.
DIRECTIONS: 3 m. E. of Ripon, S. of the road which passes through Sharow and W. of its junction with the A1.

This henge monument is similar in plan to the one on *Hutton Moor*, with two opposed entrances facing north and south. It has been heavily damaged by the plough. It should be considered as part of a larger concentration of religious sites including the *Thornborough Circles* and henge monuments on *Hutton Moor* and at *Nunwick*.
See also Chapter Three.

CASTLE STEADS

HILL-FORT
DATE: 300 B.C.–A.D. 100
MAP REF.: NZ/112075
DIRECTIONS: 6¾ m. S.E. of Barnard Castle, just over ½ m. S.W. of Dalton.

The site is well chosen for its natural defences. It lies on a steep-sided spur between two streams. The defences have been completed with a stone-built rampart with outer ditch enclosing an area of 3¾ acres. Remains of a counterscarp bank can be seen in places.

CATTERICK BRIDGE

ROMAN TOWN
DATE: Late first century–fifth century A.D.
MAP REF.: SE/220990
PUBLICATION: E. J. W. Hildyard, 'Cataractonium, Fort and Town', *Yorkshire Archaeological Journal*, XXXIX, 224–65.
DIRECTIONS: 3 m. S.E. of Richmond. Take the B6271 to Brompton, then follow the B6272 and turn right for Catterick Bridge. The Roman town lies on either side of the new road just S. of the river.

The Roman town of Cataractonium. The earliest occupation on the site seems to have been a military fort covering an area of approximately 2¼ acres. From its ditch have been recovered pieces of waterlogged wood and leather, including fragments of tents, boots and shoes.

By the early part of the second century the main east to west road across the town had been constructed and remains of timber-built shops and workshops have been found along it. A larger building with stone foundations contained a bath-house and fountain.

During the earlier half of the third century some of the shops were rebuilt in stone and about the middle of the century a town wall was added. Considerable rebuilding took place in the following century and the town continued to flourish into the fifth century. The Catterick buckle (fig. 45) was found with fourth-century pottery.

See Chapter Seven.

CAWTHORN CAMPS

ROMAN MILITARY PRACTICE CAMPS
DATE: Late first or early second century A.D.
MAP REF.: SE/784900
PUBLICATION: I. A. Richmond, 'The Four Roman Camps at Cawthorn, in the North Riding of Yorkshire', *Archaeological Journal*, LXXXIX, 17–78.
DIRECTIONS: 4 m. N. of Pickering on the edge of the Tabular Hills. Take the A170 from Pickering to Wrelton, then turn right up the road to Cawthorn. The camps are less than 1 m. N.E. of Cawthorn.

The camps are unique in Britain. The four camps were built, probably by the Ninth Legion from York, on two separate occasions. In each case one of the camps served as living-quarters for the troops while the other was being built during practice exercises.

See Chapter Seven and fig. 42.

CROWN END

CAIRNS, WALLS AND ENCLOSURE
DATE: Uncertain
MAP REF.: NZ/668075
DIRECTIONS: On Westerdale Moor, 1½ m. W.S.W. of Castleton, 6½ m. S.E. of Guisborough.

Stone walls and field plots can be seen here, and there is a circular stone-built enclosure about 129 feet in diameter with two opposed entrances facing north-east and south-west. There are also slight traces of an earthwork running across the spur to the west.

At least 200 small cairns are scattered along the spur, but, as on *Danby Rigg, Iron Howe* and other sites in Yorkshire, their date and purpose is still unknown.

DANBY RIGG

ROUND CAIRNS, STONE CIRCLE, EARTH-WORKS AND FIELDS
DATE: See below
MAP REF.: Around NZ/710065
DIRECTIONS: 1 m. S. of Danby station, 8½ m. S.E. of Guisborough.

Two earthworks cut across the spur. The more southerly, known as the 'Double Dike', is formed by three banks and two ditches. Seven hundred yards to the north, the second is a simple bank of stones. In the area between the two ditches lies a stone circle about 70 feet in diameter and some small stone cairns. The main concentration of these small cairns lies, however, to the north of the single dike. There are about 800 of these cairns on the spur, but their date and purpose is still not known.

Among the small cairns at the northern end of the spur is a standing stone, 5 feet high. This is all that remains of a stone circle, once set within a circular bank of earth, 42 feet in diameter. Two collared urns were found at the centre of the circle in the nineteenth century. There are also two normal round barrows amongst the smaller cairns at the northern end of the spur.

Several field banks can be made out on the slopes of the spur.

The stone circles and two normal-sized round barrows are all likely to be of Middle Bronze Age date. The earthworks and field banks are probably Late Bronze Age or Iron Age.

EAST AYTON

LONG BARROW
DATE: 2500–1600 B.C.
MAP REF.: TA/000864
PUBLICATION: Lord A. D. Conyngham, 'Account of Discoveries made in Barrows near Scarborough', *Journal of the British Archaeo-logical Association*, IV, 104–5.
DIRECTIONS: 2¾ m. S.W. of Scarborough, 1 m. N.E. of East Ayton in Ayton East Field, 1 m. N.W. of the road from East Ayton to Scarborough (B1262).

The barrow is about 85 feet long and is 3 feet high at its northern end. No side ditches are visible. A stone cairn was found within the mound sur-rounded by a kerb of large stones. The rubble on top of this cairn showed clear signs of burning and mixed with it were fragments of pottery, animal and human bones. Beneath the cairn lay two heaps of human bones and with each lay a 'flint arrowhead'.

At a depth of 8 inches below the surface of the barrow and near its centre lay a flat stone. This partially covered a small quantity of human bones accompanied by five lozenge-shaped arrowheads, four flint axes, two flint knives, two boars'-tusk blades and an antler macehead. This deposit, which may have been added to the mound after its completion, includes many of the tools and implements typical of the late neolithic period.
See Chapter Three.

ESTON NAB

PROMONTORY FORT
DATE: *c.* 300 B.C.–A.D. 100
MAP REF.: NZ/568184
PUBLICATION: F. Elgee, *Early Man in North East Yorkshire* (1930), 152–6.
DIRECTIONS: About 1 m. S. of Lazenby, ¾ m. E. of Eston, 3 m. N.W. of Guisborough.

A steep cliff forms a natural defence on the north-west side. The fort has been completed by constructing a bank and ditch round the southern and eastern sides to enclose an area of roughly 2½ acres. A counterscarp bank is also visible in places.

Elgee found several cremations, flint implements and fragments of a food vessel within the area of the camp, but the fort itself was probably built in the Iron Age.
See Chapter Six.

FLAT HOWE

ROUND BARROW
DATE: 1400–1000 B.C.
MAP REF.: NZ/855046
DIRECTIONS: 4½ m. S.W. of Whitby, 1¾ m. E.S.E. of Grosmont, ¼ m. W. of the Whitby-Pickering road (A169).

The barrow is encircled by a ring of stones. There is no record of the barrow having been excavated.

GOLDSBOROUGH

SIGNAL STATION
DATE: Late fourth century A.D.
MAP REF.: NZ/835152
PUBLICATION: W. Hornsby and J. D. Laverick, 'A Roman Signal Station at Goldsborough', *Archaeological Journal*, LXXXIX, 203–19.
DIRECTIONS: 4½ m. N.W. of Whitby, ¾ m.

N.N.W. of Goldsborough, about ½ m. from the sea. Take the A174 from Whitby, turn right just beyond Lythe for Goldsborough. The site lies E. of the footpath from Goldsborough to Kettleness.

This is the best preserved of the Roman signal stations along the Yorkshire coast. The tower was a wooden construction, once probably 90–100 feet high, set on stone foundations. This stood within a courtyard surrounded by a wall, 4 feet thick at the base with rounded corners strengthened by circular turrets. The gateway was set in the southern wall. The whole structure was surrounded by a ditch separated from the outer wall by a berm.

This signal station, like others along the coast, was destroyed in the early fifth century A.D.
See Chapter Seven.

HIGH BRIDESTONES

STONE CIRCLE
DATE: 1600–1000 B.C.
MAP REF.: NZ/850046
DIRECTIONS: 5 m. S.W. of Whitby on Sleights Moor, S. of the road leading from Grosmont to the main Whitby-Pickering road (A169).

There were once two stone circles here, but many of the stones have now fallen. Three stones of each circle are still standing; the largest, now badly weathered, is 7 feet high. Other single standing stones can also be seen in the neighbourhood.

HUTTON MOOR

HENGE MONUMENT
DATE: 2000–1500 B.C.
MAP REF.: SE/353735
PUBLICATION: N. Thomas, 'The Thornborough Circles near Ripon, North Riding', *Yorkshire Archaeological Journal*, XXXVIII, 425–45.
DIRECTIONS: 2½ m. N.E. of Ripon, about ¾ m. W. of the A1.

Henge monument similar in plan to the *Thornborough circles*, but more heavily damaged by the plough. Unlike the Thornborough henges, the opposed entrances face north and south. Together with the henges at *Cana* and *Nunwick*, this monument should be considered as forming part of a larger religious centre between the Rivers Ure and Swale.
See Chapter Three.

IRON HOWE

HUT CIRCLES, CAIRNS AND STONE WALLS
DATE: Uncertain
MAP REF.: SE/527951
PUBLICATION: *A History of Helmsley, Rievaulx and District* (1964), written by members of the Helmsley and Area Group of the Yorkshire Archaeological Society, p. 39 and fig. V.
DIRECTIONS: 9 m. N.W. of Helmsley, on the southern tip of Cow Rigg, between Parci Gill and Arnsgill on Snilesworth Moor.

Over 300 small stone cairns can be found clustering at the northern end of the spur and along its western and eastern flanks. Amongst the cairns lie stretches of rough stone walling. There are also two apparent hut circles on the north-east edge of the spur.

KEPWICK

LONG BARROW
DATE: 2500–1700 B.C.
MAP REF.: SE/492904
PUBLICATION: W. Greenwell, *British Barrows* (1877), 509–10.
DIRECTIONS: 6¼ m. N.E. of Thirsk, 1¼ m. E.S.E. of Kepwick on Little Moor.
The barrow is 114 feet long and 4 feet high. Five disarticulated skeletons were found between 15 and 25 feet from the eastern end, spread out along the central axis of the barrow.

LOOSE HOWE

ROUND BARROW
DATE: *c.* 1700–1400 B.C.
MAP REF.: NZ/703008
PUBLICATION: H. W. and F. Elgee, 'An Early Bronze Age Burial in a Boat-shaped Wooden Coffin from North East Yorkshire', *Proceedings of the Prehistoric Society*, XV, 87–106.
DIRECTIONS: 4¾ m. S. of Danby, on Danby High Moor.

Two burials were discovered in this mound. The earlier lay within a boat-shaped wooden coffin accompanied by a dugout canoe. At a later date a second burial had been placed in the mound. This was a cremation which had been placed within an early collared urn together with a fine stone battle-axe, a bronze dagger, a bronze pin and a pygmy cup. These objects date this later burial to the second part of the Wessex Culture, between 1550 and 1400 B.C.
See Chapter Four.

MAIDEN CASTLE

EARTHWORK AND ROUND BARROW
DATE: Uncertain
MAP REF.: SE/023981
DIRECTIONS: 11 m. W. of Richmond, 1¼ m. S.W. of Reeth, just over ½ m. S. of the B6270 and S. of the River Swale.

The site consists of a circular bank with external ditch enclosing an area about 300 feet across. The entrance faces east and is approached by a long avenue of tumbled dry-stone walling. Just north of where the avenue begins lies a large round barrow.

MALTON

ROMAN FORT
DATE: First–fifth century A.D.
MAP REF.: SE/791718
PUBLICATION: P. Corder, 'The Defences of the Roman Fort at Malton', *Roman Malton and District Report, no.* 2 (1930).
DIRECTIONS: The Roman fort lies in the angle formed by the Old Malton Road (A169 to Pickering) and the railway line, on the N.E. side of Malton.

Probably the Roman Derventio. The Ninth Legion had a camp here covering 22 acres before moving into permanent accommodation at York. The first fort, however, was built under Agricola about A.D. 79 with turf ramparts. Under Trajan these were rebuilt in stone. For the whole of its life the fort had close connexions with the civil vicus at Norton.

The fort was damaged in the Northern rising of A.D. 196, but was reconstructed, and in the third century became a storage centre for much of the corn produced on the villa estates of the Wolds. This store was burnt during the troubles at the end of the century. After a short evacuation the fort was reoccupied and infant burials suggest that the civilian population actually living in the fort was now considerable.

In the late fourth century Malton housed a force of cavalry which, when alerted by the coastal signal stations, could be sent to deal with any threatened raid.
See Chapter Seven.

SCAMRIDGE

LONG BARROW
DATE: 2500–1700 B.C.
MAP REF.: SE/892861

PUBLICATION: W. Greenwell, *British Barrows*
(1877), 484–7.

DIRECTIONS: 2 m. N.N.W. of Ebberston, less
than ½ m. N.W. of High Scamridge Farm.

The barrow is 165 feet long and is 8 feet high at
its eastern end. Fourteen disarticulated skeletons
were found spread over an area of 40 feet down
the centre of the barrow. The barrow seems to
have been constructed, like the *Willerby Wold* long
barrow, to include a crematorium trench along
which the burials had been laid. Though clear
traces of burning were found and part of the
rubble had been turned to lime, the cremation in
this barrow was incomplete.

SCARBOROUGH, CASTLE HILL

SETTLEMENT AND SIGNAL STATION
DATE: 550 B.C. and late fourth century A.D.
MAP REF.: TA/052892
PUBLICATIONS: R. A. Smith, 'Pre-Roman
Remains at Scarborough', *Archaeologia*, LXXVII,
179–200. R. G. Collingwood, *Roman Signal
Station on Castle Hill, Scarborough* (1925).
DIRECTIONS: On Castle Hill.

Nothing can now be seen of the Early Iron Age
settlement. No structures were found, but a
number of pits were excavated. These had originally been storage pits, dug to hold grain. After a
few years this type of storage pit becomes sour
and they were then filled up with rubbish from
the settlement.

The Roman signal station was similar in plan
to the better-preserved example at *Goldsborough*.
It consisted of a square tower set within a courtyard defended by a stone wall with rounded
bastions at each corner. A berm separated this
wall from the outer ditch. Like the other signal
stations along the coast, the Scarborough station
was probably destroyed at the beginning of the
fifth century.

See Chapters Six and Seven.

SHOOTING HOUSE RIGG

EARTHWORKS AND CAIRNS
DATE: Uncertain
MAP REF.: NZ/905025
DIRECTIONS: 5¼ m. S. of Whitby, W. of the
Whitby–Pickering road (A171) and S. of the
junction with the B1416.

Over 1,200 small stone cairns can be seen on the
spur and, as on *Danby Rigg* and elsewhere, their
date and purpose are still unknown.

Amongst the cairns an earthwork, comprising a
system of four banks and three ditches, cuts across
the spur. Each bank once held a row of upright
stones. These earthworks may date to the Bronze
Age.

STANDING STONES RIGG

STONE CIRCLE
DATE: 1600–1000 B.C.
MAP REF.: SE/983969
DIRECTIONS: 6 m. N.W. of Scarborough, on
Stubbs' Low Moor, about 2 m. N.W. of Clough-
ton, a few yards W. of the Scarborough-Whitby
road (A171).

The circle once contained at least twenty-four
stones and is about 32 feet across. Four cup-and-
ring-marked stones were removed from the centre
of the circle and are now in Scarborough Museum.
These may once have been associated with a
burial.

STANWICK

FORTIFICATIONS
DATE: First century A.D.
MAP REF.: NZ/180115
PUBLICATION: R. E. M. Wheeler, 'The
Stanwick Fortifications', *Society of Antiquaries of
London, Research Report*, no. XVII (1954).
DIRECTIONS: 3¼ m. S.W. of Piercebridge.
Take the B6274 from Richmond as far as Forcett,
then turn right towards Aldborough. Some of the
fortifications can be seen on either side of the road
about 1 m. before the village.

The fortifications were constructed by the
Brigantes during the first century A.D. as a centre
for anti-Roman resistance. There were three main
building phases.

The first fortification enclosed an area of 17
acres, known as 'the Tofts', south of Stanwick
church, and south of the Mary Wild Beck.

A further 130 acres to the north were enclosed
in the second phase. This incorporated a stretch
of the Beck as the only defence along part of the
southern side.

In the final phase the fortifications enclosed
over 700 acres, giving ample pasture for cattle
and sheep within the defended area.

Part of the fortifications are in the guardian-
ship of the Ministry of Public Building and
Works.

See Chapter Six and fig. 35.

STAR CARR

CAMP SITE

DATE: *c.* 7500 B.C.

MAP REF.: TA/027809

PUBLICATION: J. G. D. Clark, *Excavations at Star Carr* (1954).

DIRECTIONS: 4¾ m. S. of Scarborough, E. of the Staxton-Seamer road (A64), near the S. bank of the River Hertford, W. of Star Carr Bridge.

Nothing can now be seen on the ground of this mesolithic camping site. The camp had been made on the edge of one of the shallow meres which still remained in the Vale of Pickering during the early post-glacial period.

A rough platform of birchwood had first been laid down. This would no doubt have supported huts, though no trace of these survived. Two trees had been set at right-angles to the platform out into the water to form a rough landing-stage. In all, the camp covered an area of approximately 240 square yards.

The camp was occupied during the winter months for several years by a group of proto-Maglemosian hunters and fishers. A large quantity of organic material was recovered from the site, including food bones, antler and bone tools and weapons and flint implements.

See Chapter One.

THOMPSON'S RIGG

CAIRNS

DATE: Uncertain

MAP REF.: SE/882922

DIRECTIONS: 7 m. N.E. of Pickering, 2¾ m. N.E. of Lockton and 1 m. S.E. of Blakey Topping.

Over a hundred small cairns can be seen clustered together along the spur. These can be compared with other groups on *Danby Rigg*, *Iron Howe* and elsewhere.

THORNBOROUGH CIRCLES

HENGE MONUMENTS AND CURSUS

DATE: 2000–1500 B.C.

MAP REF.: SE/285795

PUBLICATION: N. Thomas, 'The Thornborough Circles near Ripon, North Riding', *Yorkshire Archaeological Journal*, XXXVIII, 425–45.

DIRECTIONS: About 1 m. N.E. of West Tanfield. The most northerly henge lies E. of the road from Nosterfield to West Tanfield before the junction near Camp House, and is planted with trees. The central henge lies N. of the road from West Tanfield to Thornborough, and the most southerly, on the S. side of this road, two fields away to the S.E.

The three henge monuments stand in line about ½ mile apart. They are circular, about 800 feet across, and each has two opposed entrances facing north-west and south-east. Originally each was defined by a bank and an inner and outer ditch, but the outer ditches are now largely filled up with plough soil. Excavations have shown that the bank was probably once covered with white gypsum brought from deposits no doubt along the River Ure.

Air photography revealed a cursus passing beneath the central henge and running over a mile in a north-east–south-west direction. When originally built this consisted of a pair of ditches, 144 feet apart, with a bank running along the inside of each ditch. The ditches are now completely obscured by plough soil, but the cursus can sometimes be picked out as two lines where the crops have grown taller due to the moisture in the ditches.

The Thornborough Circles should be considered as part of a larger concentration of religious sites including the henge monuments to the south-east on *Hutton Moor*, at *Nunwick* and at *Cana*. Many round barrows can also be seen clustering round these monuments.

See also Chapter Three.

WADE'S CAUSEWAY

ROMAN ROAD. *See Wheeldale Moor.*

WHEELDALE MOOR

ROMAN ROAD

DATE: *c.* late first century A.D.

MAP REF.: SE/806977

PUBLICATION: R. H. Hayes and J. G. Rutter, 'Wade's Causeway' (1964), *Research Report no. 4 of the Scarborough and District Archaeological Society*.

DIRECTIONS: 18 m. S.W. of Whitby. Follow the main Whitby-Pickering road (A169) and then fork right about 4 m. S. of Sleights along the road to Goathland. Walk S. along the West Beck to the ford at Wheeldale Bridge. From this point the Roman road can be followed running southwards. About a mile of the road is maintained by the Ministry of Public Building and Works. This section is part of Wade's Causeway, which runs from Amotherby, north-west of Malton, across

the Vale of Pickering to Cawthorn, then over the moors to Eskdale and perhaps Whitby. The road cannot now be traced north of the Esk.
See Chapter Seven.

WEST RIDING

ALDBOROUGH

ROMAN TOWN
DATE: First century–fifth century A.D.
MAP REF.: SE/406664
PUBLICATION: J. N. L. Myres, K. A. Steer, and Mrs A. M. H. Chitty, 'The Defences of Isurium Brigantum (Aldborough)', *Yorkshire Archaeological Journal*, XL, 1–77.
DIRECTIONS: 1 m. E.S.E. of Boroughbridge, E. of the main York-Boroughbridge road (A167).

Much of the site of the regional capital of the Brigantes, Isurium Brigantum, lies under the modern village, but two mosaic pavements and part of the town wall are maintained by the Ministry of Public Building and Works. Two mosaic pavements can be seen in the garden behind the Aldborough Arms.

The first occupation may well have been a military fort, but no positive evidence for this has yet been found.

By the later half of the second century stone walls made of rubble and faced with local sandstone had enclosed a roughly rectangular area of 55 acres. Four rectangular internal towers were attached to the wall, one at each of the southern angles, the other two being placed at equal distances between the south-west angle and the south gate. A berm separated this wall from the external ditch.

During the fourth century there was considerable rebuilding in the town and the defences were also reorganized. The wall was now given large angle-bastions and smaller internal bastions. A new ditch was cut and the north gate was partially blocked. Many of the mosaic pavements found in the town belong to this fourth-century phase.

The town seems to have continued to flourish to the end of the century and perhaps into the next.
See Chapter Seven.

ALMONDBURY

HILL-FORT
DATE: *c.* 300 B.C.–A.D. 100
MAP REF.: SE/153141

PUBLICATION: W. J. Varley, 'The Hill-Forts of the Welsh Marches', *Archaeological Journal*, CV, 46–48.
DIRECTIONS: On Castle Hill, 1¾ m. S.E. of the centre of Huddersfield.

The fort shows four main stages of development:

I. A relatively small fort was first built, occupying the south-western end of the summit plateau. The single bank was made of earth, faced on both sides with stone. Outside it a V-shaped ditch was dug. A single entrance was made in the north-east side opening on to the summit plateau. The sides of this entrance are slightly inturned.

II. The fort was extended to include the whole of the summit plateau, an area of approximately 8 acres. This was defended by a stone-faced earthen bank, similar to the earlier rampart, with a ditch and counterscarp bank. The single entrance lay at the north-eastern tip of the fort, and was approached up the hillside by a hollow way. Outlying banks enclosed further ground on the north-eastern slopes of the hill, including a rectangular 'annexe'.

III. In this phase the main inner rampart was rebuilt and strengthened with timber lacing, but the general plan of the fort remained the same.

IV. In the final phase the area enclosed was almost doubled by building two banks and ditches following the contours of the hill further down its slope. The entrance through these latest defences lies at the south-western end, but the only way into the inner earthwork remained by way of the entrance at the north-east end.

This latest building phase probably dates to the end of the first century B.C.

BLACKSTONE EDGE

ROMAN ROAD
DATE: Probably second century A.D.
MAP REF.: SD/973170
PUBLICATION: I. D. Margary, *Roman Roads in Britain*, Vol. II (1957).
DIRECTIONS: 2. m. E.N.E. of Littleborough, E. of the Halifax-Littleborough road (A58) where this turns S. round Cowberry Hill.

The Roman road can be made out as a green strip in the moorland rising to the top of Blackstone Edge. Near the top of the Edge the road is now exposed. It is 16 feet wide and paved with slabs set between kerbstones. Down the centre of the road runs a line of large flat stones with a central groove showing obvious signs of wear. The slope is very steep and this central groove probably took the brake pole of the carts when descending the hill. As the ground flattens out this central groove disappears and the central slabs become quite flat.

BRADLEY MOOR

LONG BARROW
DATE: 2000–1600 B.C.
MAP REF.: SE/009476
PUBLICATION: A. Butterfield, 'Structural Details of a Long Barrow on Black Hill, Bradley Moor, West Yorkshire', *Yorkshire Archaeological Journal*, XXXIV, 223–7.
DIRECTIONS: 5 m. N.W. of Keighley, 1 m. N. of Kildwick on Black Hill, right of the road from Kildwick to Low Bradley.

The barrow is 230 feet long and rises to a maximum height of 8 feet at its eastern end. It contained a stone cist, 60 feet from the eastern end. Cremated bones were found within the cist and beneath its flooring slabs a few crushed but unburnt bones. The mound contained a number of standing stones, but none of these formed a second cist. The barrow may represent a degenerate example of a megalithic chambered tomb.

A round barrow can also be seen about 100 feet to the south.
See Chapter Two.

BRADUP BRIDGE

STONE CIRCLE
DATE: 1600–1000 B.C.
MAP REF.: SE/090440
PUBLICATION: A. Raistrick, 'The Bronze Age in West Yorkshire', *Yorkshire Archaeological Journal*, XXIX, 356.
DIRECTIONS: 2½ m. N.E. of Keighley on the W. side of the Keighley-Ilkley road in Brass Castle pasture, S.W. of Bradup Bridge.

Twelve stones remain in this badly damaged circle, which measures about 30 feet across. The stones are of local millstone grit. Several seem to have been removed from the site to repair Bradup Bridge.
See Chapter Five.

DEVIL'S ARROWS

STANDING STONES
DATE: 2000–1500 B.C.
MAP REF.: SE/391666
PUBLICATION: *Proceedings of the Society of Antiquaries of London*, 2nd Series, VII, 134–8.
DIRECTIONS: On the S.W. side of Boroughbridge.

One of the most famous field monuments in Yorkshire. Three large standing stones, now naturally weathered into a fluted shape at the top. The stones stand almost in line, 200 and 370 feet apart.
See Chapter Three and fig. 17.

DOWKERBOTTOM CAVE

INHABITED CAVE
DATE: First–fourth century A.D.
MAP REF.: SD/952689
PUBLICATION: J. W. Jackson in *British Caving* (1953), 181, 235.
DIRECTIONS: 5½ m. N.W. of Grassington, 1¾ m. N.W. of Kilnsey, W. of the road from Kilnsey to Kettlewell (B6160).

The cave was occupied during the Roman period. Finds include pottery, coins, bronze needles and brooches, objects of bone and two spindle whorls of Samian ware. Burials were also made in the cave.
See also Victoria Cave and Chapter Seven.

EDBOLTON CAVE

INHABITED CAVE
DATE: 2000–1000 B.C.
MAP REF.: SE/008616
PUBLICATION: N. Newbigin, 'The Neolithic Pottery of Yorkshire', *Proceedings of the Prehistoric Society*, III, 216.
DIRECTIONS: 1¾ m. S. of Grassington, ¼ m. W. of Thorpe, S. of the road from Thorpe to Cracoe.

Sherds of Peterborough Ware, food vessel and collared urn show that the cave was used, if only for temporary shelter, during the late neolithic and earlier part of the Bronze Age. At a later date burials were made in the cave.

GRASSINGTON

HUT CIRCLES AND FIELDS
DATE: *c.* second century B.C.–fourth century A.D.
MAP REF.: SD/995655–SE/005655
PUBLICATION: A. Raistrick, 'Prehistoric Cultivations at Grassington, Yorks.', *Yorkshire Archaeological Journal*, XXXIII, 166–74.

DIRECTIONS: About 1 m. N. of Grassington, mainly on High Close, Lea Green and Sweetside.

Several types of fields can be seen. On the highest ground, on High Close and Sweetside, the fields are regular and rectangular, 350–400 feet long and about 75 feet wide. The banks separating the fields are up to 3 feet high. Several hut circles can be made out associated with the fields.

South of Bank Lane the fields are smaller and less regular. Several enclose small rectangular or circular hut enclosures.

On Lea Green the fields are large and form broad rectangles, 200–300 feet wide and 500 feet long. Amongst these can be seen oval and circular hut enclosures 50–100 feet across.

At the northern end of Lea Green there is a well-defined village of stone hut circles, clustered together within a rough stone wall. Objects recovered from this village include iron knives, bronze tweezers and pins, bone pins and a bone spoon as well as pottery and spindle whorls. These can be compared to finds made in the *Dowker-bottom* and *Victoria Caves*.

GRUBSTONES CIRCLE

STONE CIRCLE. *See Ilkley Moor.*

HORNCLIFFE CIRCLE

STONE CIRCLE. *See Ilkley Moor.*

ILKLEY MOOR

ROCK CARVINGS, STONE CIRCLES AND CAIRNS
DATE: 1700–1000 B.C.
MAP REF.: See below
PUBLICATION: A. Raistrick, 'The Bronze Age in West Yorkshire', *Yorkshire Archaeological Journal*, XXIX, 357 ff.
DIRECTIONS: On the moorland S. of Ilkley.

Rock Carvings

Rock carvings are numerous on the moorland, but tend to cluster into groups. The most common carvings are 'cup' and 'ring' marks, but on some surfaces these are joined together by wandering and enclosing lines (*see* fig. 21). One of the best examples is the *Panorama Stone* which can be seen in Ilkley, in the public gardens opposite St Margaret's Church. Another famous carved rock is the *Swastika Stone* on Addingham High Moor (SE/094470), though this may date to the Iron Age.

Stone Circles

There are five stone circles on the moor. Twelve stones remain of the *Twelve Apostles Circle* (SE/126451), though most of these are no longer standing upright. They were set in a stone and earth bank some 52 feet across.

A second circle near *Horncliffe* House on Hawksworth Moor (SE/134435) is more oval in plan, with a diameter at its widest part of 43 feet. Forty-six of the stones can still be seen set close together. Part of an inner circle can also be seen and it is possible that a burial had been made at the centre of the circle.

Twenty stones of the *Grubstones Circle* (SE/136447) survive, set edge to edge in a low earthen bank. Shooting butts have unfortunately destroyed about a third of the circle on its southern side.

Cairns

A number of cairns can also be seen on the moors. A good example, standing about 5 feet high and 85 feet across, is known as the *Skirtful of Stones* and can be found to the south-east of the Grubstones Circle.

INGLEBOROUGH

HILL-FORT
DATE: 300 B.C.–A.D. 100
MAP REF.: SD/742746
PUBLICATION: A. Raistrick, 'Iron Age Settlements in West Yorkshire', *Yorkshire Archaeological Journal*, XXXIV, 124–5.
DIRECTIONS: 8 m. N.W. of Settle, 3m. N.E. of Ingleton, E. of the Ingleton–Hawes road (B6255).

The whole summit plateau, about 15 acres in extent, is defended by a massive stone wall, now collapsed in many places. Large upright slabs were used in some places to face the wall internally. The main entrance to the fort seems to have been on the western side. Inside the fort the remains of stone hut circles can still be seen.

NUNWICK

HENGE MONUMENT
DATE: 2000–1500 B.C.
MAP REF.: SE/323748
PUBLICATION: D. P. Dymond, 'The "Henge" Monument at Nunwick, near Ripon. 1961 Excavation', *Yorkshire Archaeological Journal*, XLI, 98–107.

DIRECTIONS: 2 m. N.N.E. of Ripon, ¼ m. N. of the hamlet of Nunwick and E. of the road from Ripon to Wath.

This henge monument was first discovered by air photography, but can still be seen on the ground as a low circular bank, in places up to 3 feet high, with an internal ditch. The monument lies mainly in two ploughed fields and is almost bisected by a hedge and farm track.

The monument is 545 feet across and has two opposed entrances facing north and south. Excavations have shown the ditch to be 45 feet wide and 5 feet 10 inches deep with a 30-foot berm separating this from the bank. Unlike the *Thornborough Circles* and the henge monuments on *Hutton Moor* and at *Cana*, the Nunwick monument has no external ditch.

See Chapter Three.

PANORAMA STONE

CARVED STONE. *See Ilkley Moor.*

SKIRTFUL OF STONES

CAIRN. *See Ilkley Moor.*

SOUTH KIRKBY

HILL-FORT
DATE: 300 B.C.–A.D. 100
MAP REF.: SE/435105
DIRECTIONS: 1¾ m. S.S.E. of Hemsworth on the western edge of South Kirkby.

The fort is roughly oval in shape and encloses an area of some 4½ acres. The defences consist of a bank and ditch, the bank surviving to a height of 8–10 feet in places. The entrance was probably on the northern side.

SWASTIKA STONE

CARVED STONE. *See Ilkley Moor.*

TWELVE APOSTLES CIRCLE

STONE CIRCLE. *See Ilkley Moor.*

WINCOBANK

HILL-FORT
DATE: First century B.C.–first century A.D.
MAP REF.: SK/378910
PUBLICATION: M. A. Cotton, 'British Camps with Timber-Laced Ramparts', *Archaeological Journal*, CXI, 87.

DIRECTIONS: Near the village of Ecclesfield, 2½ m. N.E. of the centre of Sheffield.

The fort is defended by a bank, ditch and counter-scarp bank, though the ditch and counterscarp no longer survive on the northern side. The bank was originally made of rubble, mixed with timber-work and faced with stone. At some stage the timberwork in the bank caught fire and the heat fused part of the rubble into a solid mass. The fort covers an area of roughly 2½ acres.

VICTORIA CAVE

INHABITED CAVE
DATE: Intermittent occupation *c.* 15000 B.C.–fourth century A.D.
MAP REF.: SD/839651
PUBLICATIONS: D. A. E. Garrod, *The Upper Palaeolithic Age in Britain* (1926). J. W. Jackson in *British Caving* (1953), 180–1, 235.
DIRECTIONS: 1¾ m. N.E. of Settle and 900 feet above the town, on the edge of Langcliffe Scar.

Part of an antler point dating to the upper palaeolithic and a mesolithic antler barbed harpoonhead have been found in the earth at the mouth of the cave. A second upper palaeolithic antler point, decorated with incised wavy lines, has been found inside the cave.

The cave was reoccupied in the Roman period. Finds include pottery, coins, bronze brooches (including the dragonesque type), bone combs and spindle whorls.

See Chapters One and Seven.

YOCKENTHWAITE

STONE CIRCLE
DATE: 1600–1000 B.C.
MAP REF.: SD/899794
PUBLICATION: A. Raistrick, 'The Bronze Age in West Yorkshire', *Yorkshire Archaeological Journal*, XXIX, 355–6.
DIRECTIONS: 6¼ m. N.W. of Kettlewell, less than ½ m. N.W. of Yockenthwaite on the northern bank of the River Wharfe.

Twenty stones form a circle about 25 feet across. Outside the circle on the north-western side are four stones forming an arc concentric to the larger circle. There is a slight mound within the circle and this may indicate a central burial.

See also Chapter Five.

Museums to Visit

To gain some impression of the lives of our prehistoric and Roman ancestors, one should not only visit the barrows and forts which they built, but see their everyday equipment, their art and their weapons. A great wealth of material is now on display in the Yorkshire museums and the staffs of these museums will gladly provide more information on other interesting sites in their neighbourhood. A list of a few of the museums well worth visiting is given below.

PLACE	MUSEUM
ALDBOROUGH	Roman Museum (Ministry of Public Building and Works): *Finds from the Roman town.*
BRADFORD	City Art Gallery and Museum: *Finds of all periods from the West Riding.*
BRIDLINGTON	Bayle Gate Museum and Sewerby Hall: *Local finds.*
CASTLEFORD	Public Library and Museum: *Includes Roman finds from Legiolium.*
DONCASTER	Museum and Art Gallery: *Local prehistoric and Roman finds.*
HUDDERSFIELD	Tolson Memorial Museum: *Includes local prehistoric material and Roman finds from Slack.*
HULL	Transport Museum: *Includes the Mortimer Collection of neolithic and Bronze Age material from barrows in East Yorkshire and Roman finds from Malton and Brough.*
ILKLEY	Manor House Museum and Art Gallery: *On the site of the Roman fort. Local prehistoric and Roman finds.*
KEIGHLEY	Art Gallery and Museum: *Local finds.*
LEEDS	City Museum: *Prehistoric and Roman finds.*
MALTON	Roman Malton Museum: *Includes Roman finds from Malton.*
MIDDLESBROUGH	Dorman Memorial Museum: *Prehistoric and Roman finds from North-East Yorkshire.*
ROTHERHAM	Museum and Art Gallery: *Includes Roman finds from Templebrough.*
SCARBOROUGH	Scarborough Museum: *Local finds of all periods including the Gristhorp coffin burial and finds from Castle Hill, Scarborough.*

SHEFFIELD	City Museum: *Includes the Bateman Collection of Bronze Age material from barrows in Derbyshire, Staffordshire and Yorkshire as well as other local prehistoric and Roman finds.*
SKIPTON	Craven Museum: *Prehistoric and Roman including finds from Elslack.*
WHITBY	Literary and Philosophical Society Museum: *Prehistoric and Roman including finds from Goldsborough.*
YORK	Yorkshire Museum: *Comprehensive collection of prehistoric material from Yorkshire and Roman finds from York.*

In addition to the museums in Yorkshire, several important local finds are now in the British Museum, London. These include the Folkton drums, the finds from Staple Howe, the Stanwick hoard, and the Greenwell and Atkinson Collections.

Index